Archit Pandey

International Sanctions

Macroeconomic effects and retaliation

Anchor Academic
Publishing

Pandey, Archit: International Sanctions. Macroeconomic effects and retaliation, Hamburg, Anchor Academic Publishing 2017

Buch-ISBN: 978-3-96067-097-1
PDF-eBook-ISBN: 978-3-96067-597-6
Druck/Herstellung: Anchor Academic Publishing, Hamburg, 2017

Bibliografische Information der Deutschen Nationalbibliothek:
Die Deutsche Nationalbibliothek verzeichnet diese Publikation in der Deutschen Nationalbibliografie; detaillierte bibliografische Daten sind im Internet über http://dnb.d-nb.de abrufbar.

Bibliographical Information of the German National Library:
The German National Library lists this publication in the German National Bibliography. Detailed bibliographic data can be found at: http://dnb.d-nb.de

Abstract

In various instances, countries, regional organizations, and the United Nations have resorted to use of sanctions as a foreign policy, as a tool for geopolitics, in order to influence the behavior of targeted states. Numerous researches and analyses have been conducted to observe and understand the effectiveness and impact of sanctions, and subsequently dismiss them as either effective, ineffective, or counterproductive to their intended objectives.

This study seeks to address the aforementioned question; in particular, whether sanctions remain to be an option as a geopolitical tool to influence the behavior of targeted states? The core of this work consists of three case studies: first, sanctions on Russian Federation (2014-present); sanctions on Iran (1979 – present, 2006, 2012 – 2016); and, US trade embargo on Cuba (1960 – present). These case studies have been analyzed from the structural point of view to understand its specifics, background, and plausible retaliation by the state. Then, the technical results achieved by the sanctions are reviewed, and their weaknesses are highlighted. Lastly, numerous relevant arguments are provided to reinforce the conclusion.

As a result, this study concludes that economic sanctions are not very practical and feasible as a geopolitical tool. While they may serve as an initial shock to the targeted country's economy, mostly, they do not succeed in fulfilling the objective of influencing the behavior of targeted states.

Key words: Sanctions, trade, embargo, economics, geopolitics, international

Table of Contents

Introduction

Sanctions: Definition, types, and reasons for placing sanctions

What are sanctions?

Individuals and entities within a country are expected and obliged to follow the set of rules and regulations within the country. These rules and regulations are usually enshrined and encoded in the form of text, and form the national law of that country. All individuals and entities resident in a particular state, unless exempted, are bound by these set of laws that well defined, and are supposed to work for running the country and for the common interests of its people.

Countries and States, on the other hand, are bound by certain obligations to each other under an umbrella term - international law. International law, as according to the United Nations, defines the legal responsibilities of States in their conduct with each other, and their treatment of the individuals within the State boundaries.[1] States might be bounded to follow these laws by signing or being part of treaties, conventions, and universally accepted human rights, that majority of the world agrees upon.

In case of *erga omnes* (applying to all) international obligations, breaching a certain obligation attracts the independent appliance of certain penalties and subsequently the obligation to repair the material prejudices that have been caused.[2] However, unlike national law - where those who violate domestic laws receive a punishment deemed appropriate by the court - international law has no explicitly defined enforcement mechanism for violations or misconduct. Nonetheless, United Nations charter, or more specifically, Article 41 under Chapter VII, covers enforcement measures not including the use of armed force that form the basis of international law.

[1] http://www.un.org/en/globalissues/internationallaw/ (access date: 29.02.2016)

[2] Al. Bolintineanu, A. Nastase, B. Aurescu (2000), *International Public Law*, Bucharest: All Beck Publishing House, p.258.

Like many other topics and terms that fall under public international law, definition of sanctions is labyrinthine at best, and while Article 41 does not explicitly uses the term *sanctions*, it does provide us with a list of punitive measures that can be taken while making it clear that the list is not exhaustive:

The Security Council may decide what measures not involving the use of armed force are to be employed to give effect to its decisions, and it may call upon the Members of the United Nations to apply such measures. These may include complete or partial interruption of economic relations and of rail, sea, air, postal, telegraphic, radio, and other means of communication, and the severance of diplomatic relations.[3]

Hence, sanctions can be succinctly defined as penalties imposed on State and non-State actors for misconduct and/or violation of their international obligations toward other States and have breached international law regulations.

Different types of sanctions

How these aforementioned penalties may be applied, and to what extent they could be exercised depends upon myriad factors – *reason* and *purpose* being two critical factors. These penalties can take a number of forms, scope, and extent.

These penalties can be unilateral – exercised by one state, or bilateral, where several states wage sanctions against one or more nations.

Accordingly, sanctions can be diplomatic, juridical, military, cultural/sport, economic and restriction in free circulation.[4]

i. Diplomatic: Breaking the diplomatic relations, expulsion of staff, suspending official visits etc.
ii. Juridical: Suspending or nullifying preexisting treaties, or preferential partnership

---

[3] http://www.un.org/en/sections/un-charter/chapter-vii/index.html (access date: 29.02.2016)
[4] A. Crăciunescu (2006), *International Public Law*, Concordia Publishing House, Arad, p. 252.

iii. Military: Enforcement of embargo on armaments (selling, supplying, transferring etc.)

iv. Cultural: Obstruction in participation in cultural or sport events

v. Economic: Restrictions imposed by a country in international commerce, in order to convince the targeted government to change its policy; they can in the forms of, among others:

- Tariffs: Imposing taxes on goods imported from the target country
- Quotas: Limiting the quantity of goods that can be imported or exported into the other country
- Embargoes: Restricting trade with the target country[5]
- Non-Tariff Barriers (NTBs): Restrictions on imported goods, more rigorous licensing and packaging requirements, product standards etc.
- Asset freeze or seizures: Preventing assets owned by the country or its individual to be sold or moved

vi. Restriction on free circulation: Interdiction for citizens of a state to enter in the other state's territory, landing or take-off of airplanes/ships belonging to the target state

Recently, there has been a growing trend towards using targeted sanctions for other purposes as well, namely: non-proliferation, counter-terrorism, democratization, and human rights.[6]

Why do we need sanctions?

While the scope and reason of exercising sanctions on another state is mentioned already, one needs to assess why we need sanctions; whether they are an effective tool in achieving our (geopolitical) objectives.

United Nations Security Council first applied voluntary sanctions on the apartheid regime in South Africa in 1963, that later became mandatory sanctions with Resolution 418 in

[5] 'Sanctions' refer to 'economic sanctions' from this point onward.

[6] Security Council Report, http://www.securitycouncilreport.org/atf/cf/%7B65BFCF9B-6D27-4E9C-8CD3-CF6E4FF96FF9%7D/special_research_report_sanctions_2013.pdf (access date: 29.02.2016)

1977. By mid 1980s, South African growth rate had halved, and the state changed its course on Apartheid within next decade.[7]

Market value of Iranian currency, Rial, crumbled after the newly imposed United Nations Resolution 1984 in June 2011. There were not any significant impact on official currency rates that were kept artificially low, however the effect on market exchange rate of USD/IRR was immediately visible. (Figure 1)

Figure 1: Iranian Real: USDIRR Official vs Market Rate (Jan'10 – Jan'12)

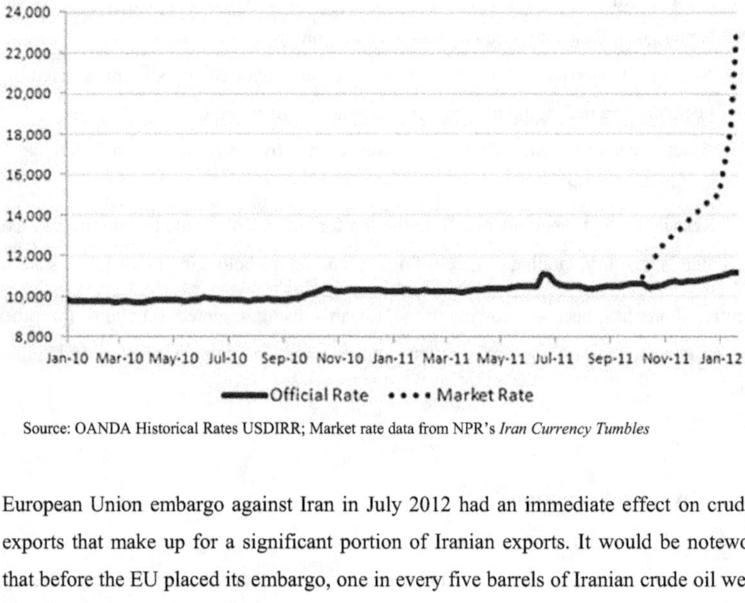

Source: OANDA Historical Rates USDIRR; Market rate data from NPR's *Iran Currency Tumbles*

European Union embargo against Iran in July 2012 had an immediate effect on crude oil exports that make up for a significant portion of Iranian exports. It would be noteworthy that before the EU placed its embargo, one in every five barrels of Iranian crude oil went to European refineries.[8] (Figure 2)

[7] Philip I. Levy (1999), *Sanctions on South Africa: What Did They Do?*, http://www.econ.yale.edu/growth_pdf/cdp796.pdf (access date: 29.02.2016)
[8] http://www.bbc.com/news/business-35317159 (access date: 29.02.2016)

Figure 2: Effect of EU sanctions on Iranian crude oil exports

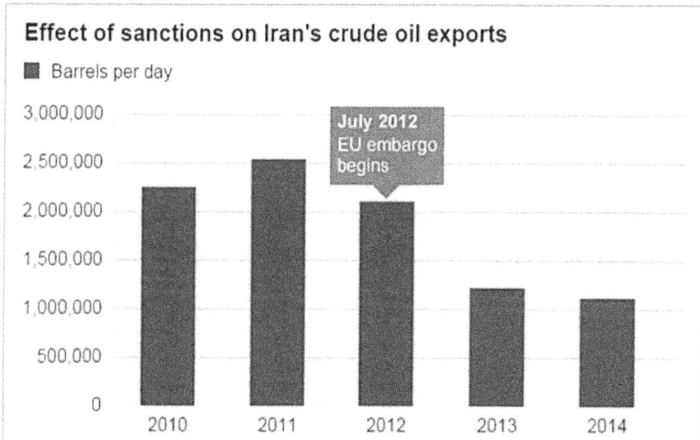

Source: OPEC

Similarly, sanctions also seemed to have impact on Russia as well. (Figure 3) However, it is noteworthy that the countries targeted by the sanctions have retaliated in a number of ways: noticeably by placing their own counter-sanctions, and/or aligning themselves with other countries.

Figure 3: Russian imports fell significantly following the EU sanctions

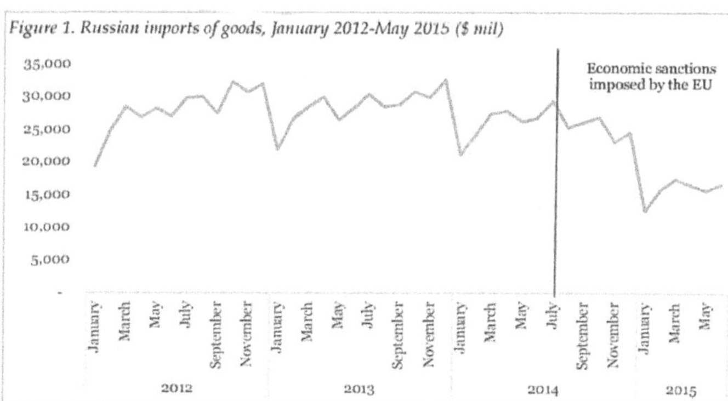

Source: Central Bank of Russia database (2015)

It is hard to delineate whether economic cost in terms of lost exports and potential jobs are always significant due to sanctions. In 2015, Russian GDP shrank by ~ 3,7%; *prima facie,* it appears that the sanctions led by the United States and European Union have had a strong impact on the economy of the country.[9] However, that also collided with more than 70% fall in oil prices around the world, which made up for a significant amount of Russian exports as a whole.

A number of economists and policy analysts also believe that economic sanctions are not an effective tool to attain intended objectives, that they merely hurt ordinary citizens and correlation between sanctions and effect on economy is indistinguishable in most of the cases.

The following cases on Russia, Iran, and Cuba, extrapolate and analyze the effect of economic sanctions on respective countries, and the macroeconomic effects that they have had on their economy as a whole. We shall dwell into each country, the background – that is, the political factors that ultimately led to sanctions being imposed on them -, and assess the impact on their respective economies and any subsequent analysis that we can draw from it.

Methodology

This study utilizes primarily quantitative method in order to assess the impact on respective economies and arrive at the conclusion. It also uses surveys to help understand perception of the people living in the country regarding the impact of the sanctions on their country, and their perception. All publicly available data has been interpreted accordingly, and cited accordingly. We have also cited work and drawn inferences, as deemed necessary, from research and publications published in eminent journals in order to draw a coherent picture and further reinforce our arguments used in this study.

---

[9] http://www.bbc.com/news/business-35398423 (access date: 29.02.2016)

Case study: Russian Federation

Impact of economic sanctions led by United States, European Union, Ukraine, Norway, Canada, Japan, South Korea, Australia, etc. on Russian Federation (March 2014 – present)

Background

On November 21, 2013, Ukraine witnessed its second major political turmoil since its independence in 1991. President Viktor Yanukovych cancelled the preparations for implantation of Association agreement with the European Union, resulting in massive protests in Kiev, the country's capital. Subsequently, a wave of demonstration swept across the country demanding integration with European Union; however, violent dispersal of protestors by the Special police on November 30th fueled this demonstration even further. These demonstrations garnered a wide support from the international community. European Union, United Nations, NATO, OSCE, along with representatives from Australia, Canada, Germany, and Poland etc. also showed their solidarity with the growing protests after the events on November 30. Russian Foreign Minister Sergey Lavrov stated, "other nations should not interfere in Ukraine's political turmoil."

Latter events saw protests against abuse of power, corruption, and a demand for change in life and political structure in Ukraine,[10] eventually resulting in ousting of the President in February 2014. Amidst a pro-EU rally, these protests – aptly named Euromaidan – took a form of social and political movement. They were further fueled by numerous demonstrations across the country, internet activism, political support by opposition parties, leading up to civil resistance and disobedience in hopes for a political revamp. However, Euromaidan also paved the way for further events that were to highlight significant social, cultural, ethnic, and linguistic divide, taking a completely different course in the country's 20-year-old post-Soviet history.

---

[10] euronews. (2016). Ukrainian opposition uses polls to bolster cause. [online] Available at: http://www.euronews.com/2013/12/13/ukrainian-opposition-uses-polls-to-bolster-cause/ [Accessed 4 May 2016].

Since its independence in 1991 from Soviet Union, Ukraine struggled with a strong, uniform Ukrainian national identity.

This is especially visible in the ethnic and linguistic division of the country. According to a 2001 census (which is the only census conducted so far in independent Ukraine), 8.3 Million people – nearly 17.3% of the population - identify themselves as (ethnic) Russians.[11] Similar data suggests that more than 29.3% of the population considers Russian to be their first language (Figure 4); however, despite a massive support, Russian-speaking minority in Ukraine forms the largest language group in Europe with its language having no official status at all. A survey conducted by Institute of Sociology, National Academy of Science of Ukraine, found that around 36.7% respondents speak Russian at home, while 25.8% speak both Russian and Ukrainian.

Figure 4: Percentage of people speaking Russian as their sole mother tongue

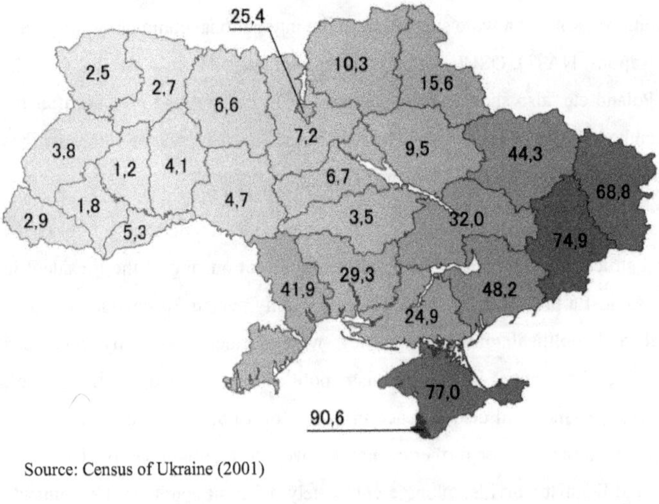

Source: Census of Ukraine (2001)

[11] 2001.ukrcensus.gov.ua. (2001). Всеукраїнський перепис населення 2001. [online] Available at: http://2001.ukrcensus.gov.ua/eng/results/general/nationality/ [Accessed 4 May 2016].

There is a clear division in the country when it comes to economic well-being. (Figure 5) It, possibly, has to do with the fact that Eastern Ukraine has major mechanical, agricultural, and metallurgical industries, while Southeastern Ukraine and Crimea are one of the most tourist destinations.

Figure 5: Average monthly salary (in UAH) in Ukraine by region (FY 2013)

Source: State Statistics Services of Ukraine (2013)

Aforementioned economic, ethnic, cultural, and linguistic divide also translate into a major political divide within the country, According to a poll by Research & Branding Group, while more than 84% Western Ukrainians supported Euromaidan, compares to less than 33% in South Ukraine and 13% in Eastern Ukraine. Plausible reasons cited for not supporting/opposing the Euromaidan were that its consequences sooner could be negative, along with further ties with Russia.[12]

[12] Rb.com.ua. (2012). Euromaydan - 2013. R&B Group. [online] Available at: http://rb.com.ua/eng/projects/omnibus/8840/ [Accessed 5 May 2016].

Pro-Russian unrest and Russian military intervention in Ukraine

Euromaidan, that started as a social and political movement and as a hope for change soon met opposition in Eastern and Southern Ukraine in the form of aptly named – Antimaidan. Yanukovych's part – Party of Regions – had a heavy political base in country's east. (Figure 6) It did not help that by now, Euromaidan itself was marred with several political alliances and extremist groups that were viewed with suspicion in Eastern and Southern Ukraine and gathered mild international criticism as well.

Figure 6: Party of Regions, 2012 elections results

Source: Ukrainian Parliamentary election results (2012)

In a poll conducted by Kyiv International Institute of Sociology in February 2014, more than 41% of respondents from Crimea, 33.2% from Donetsk Oblast, 24.1% of Lugansk Oblast and 13-16% respondents in Dnipropetrovsk, Kharkiv, and Odessa supported a union between Ukraine and Russia.[13] Another poll led by International Republican Institute found that 26-27% of respondents in southern and eastern Ukraine viewed Euromaidan as coup d'état; more than 67% in eastern Ukraine and 52% in southern Ukraine opposed joining NATO, and 72% answered that they thought the country was heading into the wrong direction.[14]

Political turmoil worsened in January-March 2014, beginning primarily with Odessa and Lugansk. On January 26, 2014, up to 2000 Euromaidan protestors marched on Regional State Administration building in an attempt to capture it, however were soon met with municipal barricades and pro-government supporters.[15] Later on in May, Odessa witnessed its worst civil conflict since 1918, where clashes and arson resulted in death of numerous pro-Russian supporters.[16]

On March 1st, council of Luhansk Oblast voted to demand giving Russian the status of second official language, disarm Euromaidan self-defense units, and ban extremist political organizations like Svoboda.[17] On March 4th, pro-Russian protestors took control of the local Regional Administration in Donetsk, elected a governor, and proclaimed more freedom to the city and structuring a new administration.[18]

On March 16, 2014, Crimea held a referendum to (re-) join Russia.[19] On March 17th, United States, European Union, and Canada placed first-round of targeted sanctions on Russia.

---

[13] Kiis.com.ua. (2014). How relations between Ukraine and Russia should look like? Public opinion polls results. [online] Available at: http://www.kiis.com.ua/?lang=eng&cat=reports&id=236&page=1 [Accessed 6 May 2016].
[14] International Republican Institute. (2014). Public Opinion Survey Residents of Ukraine. [online] Available at:http://www.iri.org/sites/default/files/2014%20April%205%20IRI%20Public%20Opinion%20Survey%20of%20Ukraine,%20March%2014-26,%202014.pdf [Accessed 5 May 2016].
[15] Комментарии.ua, (2014). Одесский горсовет приготовился к штурму. [online] Available at: http://odessa.comments.ua/news/2014/01/26/214700.html [Accessed 7 May 2016].
[16] Kyiv Post, (2014). What really happened in Odessa. [online] Available at: http://www.kyivpost.com/article/content/ukraine/what-really-happened-in-odessa-a-step-by-step-reconstruction-of-a-tragedy-that-killed-46-people-video-346192.html [Accessed 7 May 2016].
[17] Украинская Правда. (2014). В Луганске участники "русской весны" захватили ОГА и просят у Путина ввести войска. [online] Available at: http://www.pravda.com.ua/rus/news/2014/03/2/7017106/ [Accessed 7 May 2016].
[18] McElroy, D. (2014). Ukraine crisis: separatist in Donetsk proclaims 'people's government'. [online] Telegraph.co.uk. Available at: http://www.telegraph.co.uk/news/worldnews/europe/ukraine/10676785/Separatist-in-Donetsk-proclaims-peoples-government.html [Accessed 7 May 2016].
[19] RT International. (2014). Crimea declares independence, seeks UN recognition. [online] Available at: https://www.rt.com/news/crimea-referendum-results-official-250/ [Accessed 8 May 2016].

Crimea and Russian military intervention

Ukraine is divided into 27 administrative divisions: 24 oblasts (provinces), Autonomous Republic of Crimea, and Kiev and Sevastopol – both having a special legal status.

Primarily since 17th century onward, Crimea was a part of Russian empire. Eventually with the rise of Soviet Union, it became a part of Russian Soviet Federative Socialist Republic (RSFSR), until it changed hands and was transferred to Ukrainian Soviet Socialist Republic in 1954 as an administrative measure. In January 1991, Crimea held its referendum titled – Referendum on sovereignty. Voters were asked whether they wanted to re-establish the Crimean Autonomous Soviet Socialist Republic (Crimea ASSR), and the proposal was approved by 94% of voters.[20] In 1992, Crimean Parliament renamed ASSR to the Republic of Crimea, proclaimed self-government, and passed the first Crimean constitution. Eventually, it agreed to remain part of Ukraine[21]; however, 1995 saw Ukrainian parliament abolishing the Crimean Constitution, and cancelling majority of laws and decrees passed earlier. Black Sea Fleet – established in 1783 – stayed loyal to Russia after the fall of Soviet Union, and Ukraine agreed to lease the naval base to Russia until 2017, which was eventually extended up to 2042.

Beginning March 2014, amidst political turmoil and civic unrest and with Crimea being an important geopolitical asset, Russian soldiers without insignia took control of strategic positions in the region. Crimean leadership announced a referendum on secession from Ukraine, which was struck immediately by the Ukrainian parliament as illegal and unconstitutional.[22] On March 16, a referendum took place that was deemed as illegal by the international community, with Russia defending it as complying with right to self-determination of people. On March 18, Republic of Crimea and City of Sevastopol were fully annexed as Crimean federal district of Russian Federation.

---

[20] Taylor, A. (2014). To understand Crimea, take a look back at its complicated history. [online] Washington Post. Available at: https://www.washingtonpost.com/news/worldviews/wp/2014/02/27/to-understand-crimea-take-a-look-back-at-its-complicated-history/ [Accessed 10 May 2016].

[21] Zakon1.rada.gov.ua. (1991). Про відновлення Кримської Автономної Радянської Соціалістичної Республіки. [online] Available at: http://zakon1.rada.gov.ua/laws/show/712-12 [Accessed 10 May 2016].

[22] Laura Smith-Spark. Phil Black and Frederik Pleitgen, C. (2014). Russia flexes military muscle as tensions rise in Ukraine's Crimea - CNN.com. [online] CNN. Available at: http://edition.cnn.com/2014/02/26/world/europe/ukraine-politics [Accessed 10 May 2016].

Referendum results posted that 96.7% voters in Autonomous Republic of Crimea and 95.6% in Sevastopol voted to join Russian Federation.[23]

Pew Research Center surveyed opinions in Ukraine and Crimea on unrest and referendum; despite international criticism and skepticism on referendum, 91% of the Crimean respondents believed that the vote was free and fair, with 88% asking the Ukrainian government to recognize the results.[24]

Donetsk and Lugansk Oblasts – together known as Donbass region – witnessed pro-government protests escalating into an armed conflict with secessionist tendencies from March 2014 onward. Self-declared Donetsk People's Republic (DPR) and Lugansk People's Republic (LPR), they were backed by Russian citizens, ultranationalists, along with heavily debated role of Russian state.[25] Insurgency and armed conflict continues to this day.

Sanctions and their extent

On March 17, a day after the Crimean referendum and in response to Russian military intervention, United States, European Union, and Canada launched first round of sanctions against certain Russian individuals and entities. Japan quickly followed, along with Australia on March 19th. Albania, Iceland, Montenegro, Moldova, and Ukraine also followed the EU and imposed travel bans on few individuals and trade restrictions. In response, Russian State Duma – the parliament – unanimously passed a resolution asking for all parliamentary members to be included in the sanctions list.[26]

---

[23] RT International. (2014). Crimea declares independence, seeks UN recognition. [online] Available at: https://www.rt.com/news/crimea-referendum-results-official-250/ [Accessed 10 May 2016].

[24] Pew Research Center. (2014). Despite Concerns about Governance, Ukrainians want to remain one country. [online] Available at: http://www.pewglobal.org/files/2014/05/Pew-Global-Attitudes-Ukraine-Russia-Report-FINAL-May-8-2014.pdf [Accessed 9 May 2016].

[25] Gibbons-Neff, T. (2015). The unusual difficulty of tracking Russia's dead in Ukraine and Syria. [online] Washington Post. Available at: https://www.washingtonpost.com/news/checkpoint/wp/2015/10/27/the-unusual-difficulty-of-tracking-russias-dead-in-ukraine-and-syria/ [Accessed 10 May 2016].

[26] All Russian MPs volunteer to be subject to US, E. (2014). All Russian MPs volunteer to be subject to US, EU sanctions. [online] Sputniknews.com. Available at: http://sputniknews.com/voiceofrussia/news/2014_03_18/All-Russian-MPs-volunteer-to-be-subject-to-US-EU-sanctions-7889/ [Accessed 10 May 2016].

In April 2014, United States and European Union further expanded their sanctions – termed as second round of sanctions.

From July 2014 onward, following the insurgency in Donbass region, US, EU, Japan, Australia, Norway, Switzerland, Canada, and Ukraine, and G7 expanded their sanctions to include major entities, more individuals, and total freeze of assets.[27] This third round of sanctions continue to this day.

To give some perspective, EU sanctions comprise of[28]:

- Diplomatic measures: EU-Russia summit cancelled; no bilateral summits to be held regularly.
- Restrictive measures: Asset freeze on more than 37 entities and 149 people, including visa bans.
- Restriction for Crimea and Sevastopol: Ban on Crimean imports; investment in Crimea prohibited; ban on providing tourism services; complete ban on providing goods and technical and brokerage services
- Economic sanctions: Restrictions on targeted cooperation and exchanges with Russia; EU nationals and companies can no longer buy/sell financial instruments in Russia; complete trade ban on numerous Russian entities; embargo on import/export of any arms and other related products and services, etc.

Based on latest announcement made in March '16, Council of the European Union planned to extend its restrictive measures until at least September 15, 2016.[29]

---

[27] BBC News. (2014). How far do EU-US sanctions on Russia go? - BBC News. [online] Available at: http://www.bbc.com/news/world-europe-28400218 [Accessed 10 May 2016].
[28] Newsroom - European Commission. (n.d.). EU sanctions against Russia over Ukraine crisis - Newsroom - European Commission. [online] Available at: http://europa.eu/newsroom/highlights/special-coverage/eu_sanctions_en [Accessed 10 May 2016].
[29] Consilium.europa.eu. (2016). Timeline - EU restrictive measures in response to the crisis in Ukraine - Consilium. [online] Available at: http://www.consilium.europa.eu/en/policies/sanctions/ukraine-crisis/history-ukraine-crisis/ [Accessed 10 May 2016].

Russian political response

On March 20 2014, Russian Foreign Ministry published sanctions against certain American politicians. List later on expanded to include 13 Canadian officials as well.[30]

On August 6 2014, President of Russian Federation Vladimir Putin signed a decree mandating an embargo on agricultural products originating from countries that adopted or joined introduction of sanctions against Russia.[31]

Eventually, Russia announced a ban on use of airspace by Ukrainian airplanes, along with entry ban on more than 89 EU politicians.

Currently, Russian embargo on products originating from countries that participated in sanctions against Russia extends until August 5, 2016.[32]

Analysis

Sanctions from both ends significantly altered the political and economic dynamics. US-EU-led sanctions targeted major Russian companies, affecting investments and trade. Russia also launched sanctions against aforementioned countries; being a major trade partner, it has had arguably a noticeable effect on their economies – or so does the rhetoric from both sides say.

For the purpose of our analysis, we shall divide our analysis into two major parts: Effect of sanctions on Russia led by US-EU, observing major macroeconomic indicators and taking into account any other factors that could have had impact on it. Next, we shall also touch on retaliation efforts by Russia, and whether it minimized the impact of US-EU led sanctions.

[30] RT International. (2014). Sanctions tit-for-tat: Moscow strikes back against US officials. [online] Available at: https://www.rt.com/news/foreign-ministry-russia-sanctions-133/ [Accessed 10 May 2016].

[31] Garant.ru. (2014). УКАЗ ПРЕЗИДЕНТА РФ ОТ 6 АВГУСТА 2014 Г. N 560 "О ПРИМЕНЕНИИ ОТДЕЛЬНЫХ СПЕЦИАЛЬНЫХ ЭКОНОМИЧЕСКИХ МЕР В ЦЕЛЯХ ОБЕСПЕЧЕНИЯ БЕЗОПАСНОСТИ РОССИЙСКОЙ ФЕДЕРАЦИИ". [online] Available at: http://www.garant.ru/hotlaw/federal/558039/ [Accessed 10 May 2016].

[32] RAPSI. (2016). Russian authorities bust 5,000 tons of sanctioned food products since November - report. [online] Available at: http://rapsinews.com/news/20160425/275948715.html [Accessed 10 May 2016].

Political commentary aside, it is difficult to analyze the impact on economy of Russia that US-EU led sanctions have had so far. Russian economy is heavily dependent upon export of minerals and oils, and oil based products. (Figure 7) In 2014 alone, it accounted for around 70% of total exports, valued at US$ 382 Billion.

Figure 7: Russian exports in 2014

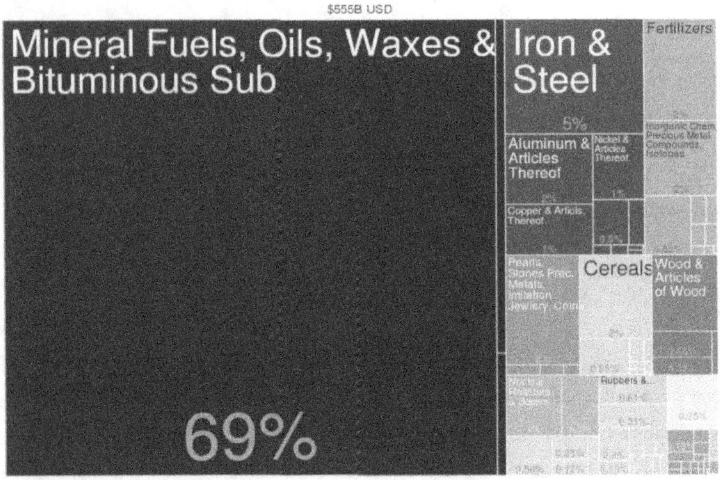

Source: The Atlas of Economic Complexity, Center for International Development, Harvard University

Subsequently, massive drop in crude oil prices from June 2014 onward had a significant impact on Russian economy. However, because the sanctions were placed not so long back in March 2014 itself, it leads to a question whether it were sanctions or global oil prices that led to a slowdown and ultimately a recession in Russian economy. Following table (Figure 8) shows an immediate slowdown in GDP growth rate Q3 2014 onward.

Figure 8: Quarterly GDP Growth Rate – Russian Federation (2013Q1 – 2015Q4)

(Numbers in red indicate period of sanctions)

Quarter	**Quarterly GDP Growth Rate (%)**
2013-Q1	0.47
2013-Q2	0.33
2013-Q3	0.32
2013-Q4	0.51
2014-Q1	0.34
2014-Q2	0.33
2014-Q3	-0.67
2014-Q4	-0.64
2015-Q1	-1.44
2015-Q2	-1.27
2015-Q3	-0.78
2015-Q4	-1.04

Source: OECD Data

Thus, it becomes critical to observe the change in GDP growth rate over a smaller period, and change in crude oil prices – main constituent of Russian exports. For this, we shall compare the Quarterly GDP growth rate with Global crude oil prices (measured in US$/Barrel), and trend lines indicating the changes. (Figure 9)

Figure 9: Quarterly GDP Growth Rate, Russia (2013Q1 – 2015Q4) vs. Crude Oil prices in the international market

Quarter	Russia	Crude Oil Prices (US$/Barrel)
2013-Q1	⇧ 0.47	⇧ 102.52
2013-Q2	⇧ 0.33	⇧ 99.74
2013-Q3	⇧ 0.32	⇧ 108.76
2013-Q4	⇧ 0.51	⇧ 105.48
2014-Q1	⇧ 0.34	⇧ 104.04
2014-Q2	⇧ 0.33	⇧ 108.37
2014-Q3	⇨ -0.67	⇧ 95.85
2014-Q4	⇨ -0.64	⇨ 60.7
2015-Q1	⇩ -1.44	⇩ 52.83
2015-Q2	⇩ -1.27	⇨ 61.31
2015-Q3	⇨ -0.78	⇩ 46.28
2015-Q4	⇩ -1.04	⇩ 36.57

Source: Commodities Market Review, World Bank; OECD

Thus, we observe a similar trend in lower oil prices and lowered quarterly GDP growth rate in Russia. However, we might want to extrapolate further and look into the impact in domestic market. For this, we would next observe the currency rate fluctuations; this is in particular noticeable for the headlines that it made during December 2014 events and uproar in Russian market that soon followed.

Falling Ruble and Central Bank intervention

Following the sanctions and lower oil prices, value of Russian currency, Ruble (RUB), dropped significantly. (Figure 10) Value of Russian Ruble as on January 1, 2013 stood at 30.15. January 2014 had a similar rate: USD/RUB = 33.68. With lower oil prices (and sanctions placed in March), USDRUB rate in August 2014 was around 36.14. It is important to note that Russian Central Bank had plans for free-floating the currency from

January 2014 itself.[33] However, the rate quickly went up from November onward, with Central Bank free-floating the currency in a controlled manner, and in December 2014 alone, Russian Ruble fell more than 50% against US Dollar.

Figure 10: USD/RUB exchange rate (January 2013 – present)

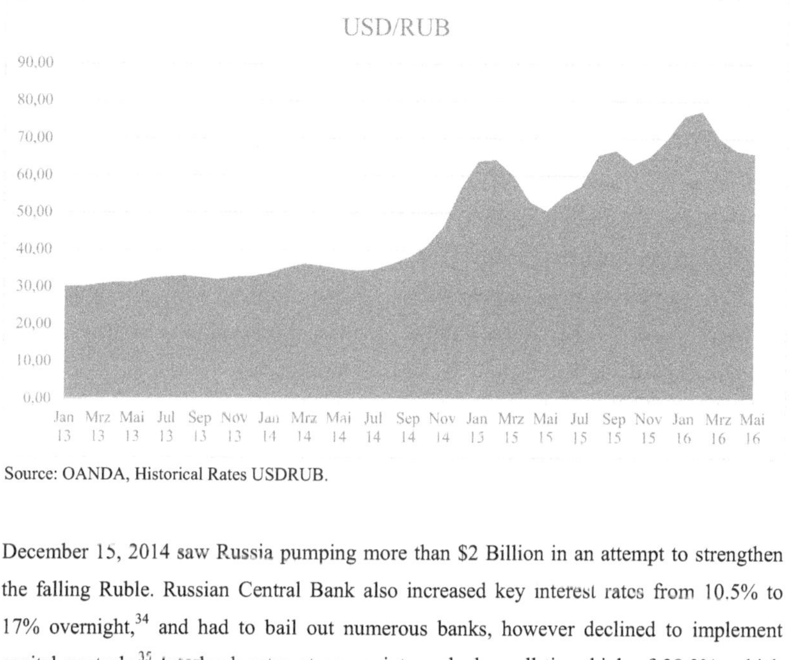

Source: OANDA, Historical Rates USDRUB.

December 15, 2014 saw Russia pumping more than $2 Billion in an attempt to strengthen the falling Ruble. Russian Central Bank also increased key interest rates from 10.5% to 17% overnight,[34] and had to bail out numerous banks, however declined to implement capital controls.[35] Interbank rates at one point reached an all-time high of 28.3%, which was even higher than the rates during 2008-9 global financial crisis. USDRUB peaked at 83.59 on January 22, 2015. Current rate, as of June 4, 2016, is 65.56.

---

[33] Ostroukh, A. (2014). Russia Ready to Float Ruble Next Year Regardless of Rate. [online] WSJ. Available at: http://www.wsj.com/news/articles/SB10001424052702304419104579326441407494108 [Accessed 12 May 2016].

[34] Bloomberg.com. (2014). Russia Defends Ruble With Biggest Rate Rise Since 1998. [online] Available at: http://www.bloomberg.com/news/articles/2014-12-15/russia-increases-key-interest-rate-to-17-to-stem-ruble-decline [Accessed 12 May 2016].

[35] Anderson, J. (2014). Ruble Crisis Is Testing Russia's Resources. [online] DealBook. Available at: http://dealbook.nytimes.com/2014/12/17/russian-government-tries-to-support-volatile-ruble/?_r=0 [Accessed 12 May 2016].

However, once again, we are posed with the same issue whether it was sanctions or a massive decline in international crude oil prices that form the country's major export that resulted in a massive decline in economy and fall in currency rate. The relationship between USDRUB and international crude oil prices would be that of an inverse relationship, since higher the international crude oil prices, the more profit it is for oil export oriented Russian economy.

To better showcase this relationship and for illustrative purposes, we look at international crude oil prices from a different angle. We shall look at the purchasing power of US$ 1000 with respect to international crude oil; the lower the oil prices, the higher would be the amount that US$ 1000 can buy. A comparison shown below (Figure 11) portrays the graph, comparing Oil prices rate from January 2014 until December 2015, and USDRUB rates for the same period. Noticeably, it results in a trend line that is quite similar. Although it does not result in a conclusive and final evidence, one could also argue as to what exactly caused the currency to drop in December 15, 2014 – full 7 months after the first round of sanctions and 4 months after the third round of sanctions against Russia.

Figure 11: USDRUB vs International Crude Oil Prices (Jan'14 – Dec'15)

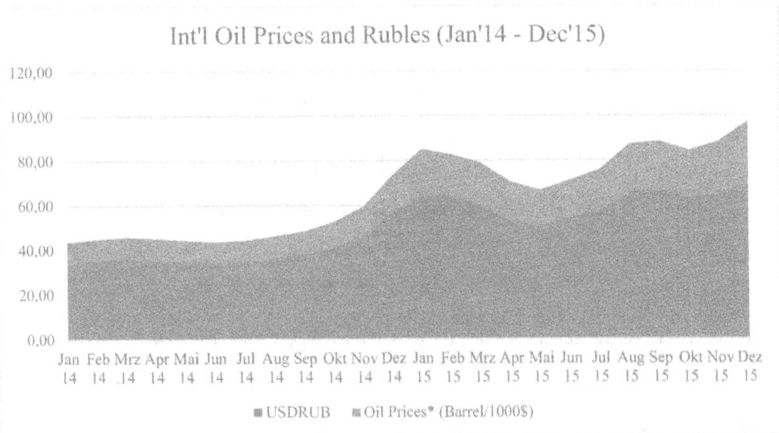

Note: * indicates how many barrels can 1000$ buy? (Higher the number, lower the international crude oil prices per US$). Source for data: OANDA, Historical Rates USDRUB; World Bank

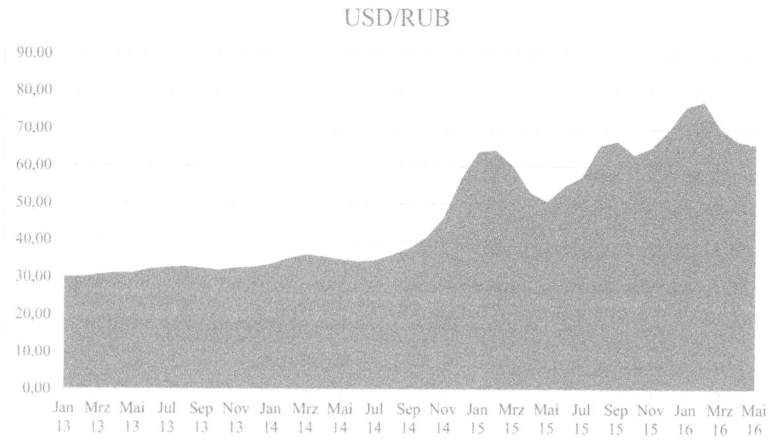

Figure 12: USDRUB, USDKZT vs International Crude Oil Prices (Jan'14 – Dec'15)

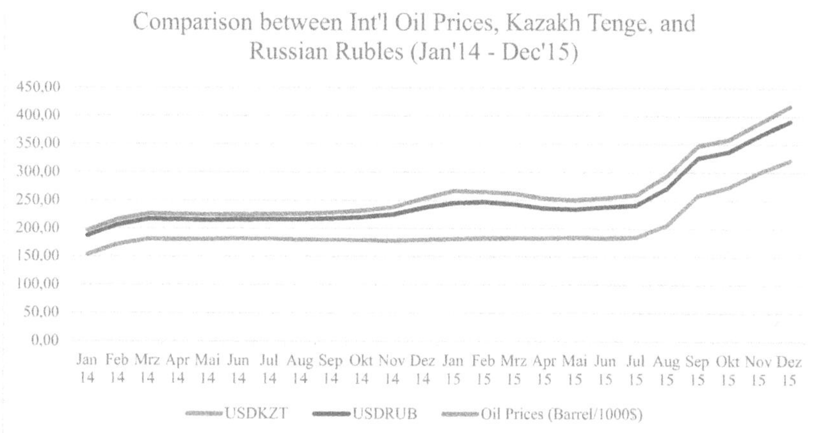

Note: * indicates how many barrels can 1000$ buy? (Higher the number, lower the international crude oil prices per US$). Source for data: OANDA, Historical Rates USDRUB, USDKZT; World Bank

Kazakhstan is another example of an oil-oriented export economy, with more than 59% of its exports being petroleum oils, natural gas etc.[36] Figure 12 above illustrates the relationship between Russian Rubles, Kazakh Tenge (KZT), and international crude oil prices. We could also observe the quarterly GDP growth rate for Kazakhstan and how it compares against quarterly GDP growth rate in Russia and international crude oil price changes. (Figure 13)

[36] Atlas.cid.harvard.edu. (2016). What did Kazakhstan export in 2014? | The Atlas Of Economic Complexity. [online] Available at: http://atlas.cid.harvard.edu/explore/tree_map/export/kaz/all/show/2014/ [Accessed 15 May 2016].

Figure 13: Quarterly GDP growth – Russia and Kazakhstan and Oil prices

Period	Quarterly GDP Growth rate %		Crude Oil Prices ($/Barrel)
	Russia	Kazakhstan	
2014Q1	⇧ 0.34	⇧ 3.8	⇧ 104.04
2014Q2	⇧ 0.33	⇧ 3.9	⇧ 108.37
2014Q3	⇨ -0.67	⇧ 4	⇧ 95.85
2014Q4	⇨ -0.64	⇧ 4.3	⇨ 60.7
2015Q1	⇩ -1.44	⇨ 2.3	⇩ 52.83
2015Q2	⇩ -1.27	⇩ 1.7	⇨ 61.31
2015Q3	⇨ -0.78	⇩ 1	⇩ 46.28
2015Q4	⇩ -1.04	⇩ 1.2	⇩ 36.57

Source: Commodities Market Review, World Bank; OECD; Agency of Statistics of Republic of Kazakhstan

Housing market

Decline in housing prices can often be an indicator that supply exceeds demand, or that prices are inflated and need to be adjusted. Decline in housing market prices could also be linked with exorbitant interest rates, when mortgage rates are too high, or when people would like to invest money elsewhere or not at all. In times of recession and weak currency, people might want to cash in on their investments instead of further investing in the real estate and shooting the prices up.

According to Federal Bureau for Government Statistics, apartment prices in Moscow oblast from year 2010-15 continue to fall. (Figure 14) This is, in part, due to after-effects of 2008-9 financial crisis, and recession in 2014-15. Russians are cutting back on spending, and in 2015, 18% fewer apartments were sold in Moscow than in 2014.[37]

[37] The Moscow Times. (2016). Moscow's Apartment Market Down 30 Percent | News. [online] Available at: http://www.themoscowtimes.com/businessrealestate/article/moscows-apartment-market-down-30-percent/556280.html [Accessed 15 May 2016].

Figure 14: Average price per square meter (in US$-exchange rate adjusted), for average quality flats in primary real estate, Moscow Oblast

	2010	2011	2012	2013	2014	2015
I Quarter	1941.38	1819.91	1842.04	1814.68	1494.47	1303.57
II Quarter	1813.04	1903.80	1789.13	1742.62	1513.07	1569.29
III Quarter	1766.03	1839.57	1740.53	1682.06	1458.73	1267.06
IV Quarter	1709.97	1719.81	1788.05	1693.35	1137.45	1277.00

Source: Federal Bureau for Government Statistics, Russian Federation http://www.gks.ru/dbscripts/cbsd/DBInet.cgi

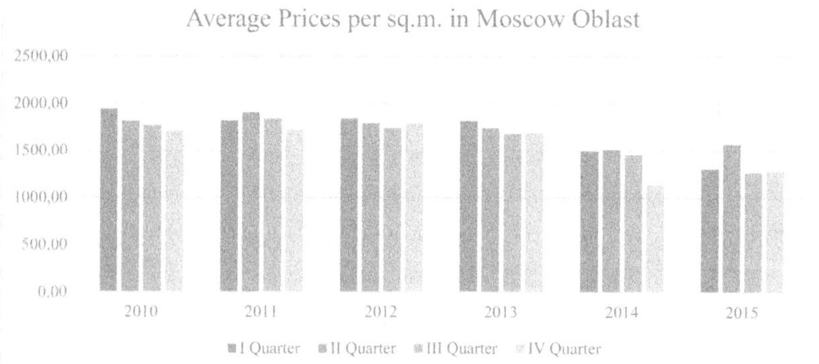

Retaliation and Conclusion

Beginning 2014 and amidst sanctions, lowering oil prices, and capital flight, Russia launched a full-scale effort to initiate or build upon trade relations with other countries that were not parties to the sanctions against Russia.

Prime examples of such efforts are growing cooperation with countries like China, and India, and pursuing more active role in pre-existing or new organizations such as Shanghai Cooperation Organization, New Development Bank (set up by BRICS), and Asia Infrastructure Investment Bank (AIIB). AIIB – joined by other leading regional powers such as China, India, South Korea, Australia etc. – holds capital that amounts to around half of World Bank.[38]

In November 2014, Russia and China signed the largest gas deal ever for Russian Oil and Gas Company – Gazprom. This US$ 400 Billion deal is regarding Power of Siberia/Altai pipeline, which is stipulated to be realized by 2018.[39] Russian oil imports have become 4 times than that of year 2010, and it is has replaced Saudi Arabia as top oil supplier to China.

Nonetheless, with economy facing a severe downturn, numerous companies suspended sales or halted their business activities in Russia. IKEA temporarily suspended its sales of goods, including Volvo, Apple, and Steam, citing high volatility a weak Ruble.[40] CEO Herman Gref, of Sberbank Rosii – one of the largest banks in Russia - stated. "that contraction of Russian economy is not just a phase but a reality to which it has to adapt, primarily due to low oil prices." Within 2015-16, real earnings dropped by 4.3%, and quarter of the banks exited the Russian market.[41]

Edward Christie Hunter, NATO's Defense Economist, writes in NATO Review magazine, "As the European economy overwhelmingly shrugs off the effects of Russia's recession – which is only partly caused by sanctions – Western Allies should take comfort in the knowledge that pursuing a strong and principled sanctions policy appears eminently affordable." Furthermore, he argues only two countries in the European Union – Sweden and Greece – experienced negative trade losses and it has been because of 'general loss in export competitiveness and not due to the Russian downturn.'[42]

---

[38] The Economist. (2014). Why China is creating a new "World Bank" for Asia. [online] Available at: http://www.economist.com/blogs/economist-explains/2014/11/economist-explains-6 [Accessed 16 May 2016].
[39] RT. (2014). Russia-China 'Gas Deal of the century'. [online] Available at: https://www.rt.com/files/news/27/14/40/00/gas3.7.jpg [Accessed 16 May 2016].
[40] Kramer, A. (2014). *Russia's Steep Rate Increase Fails to Stem Ruble's Decline*. [online] Nytimes.com. Available at: http://www.nytimes.com/2014/12/17/business/russia-ruble-interest-rates.html [Accessed 19 May 2016].
[41] РБК. (2016). «Новая реальность»: о чем Герман Греф рассказал акционерам Сбербанка. [online] Available at: http://www.rbc.ru/finances/27/05/2016/574835599a7947103afd8ece [Accessed 19 May 2016].
[42] Christie, E. (2015). Sanctions after Crimea: Have they worked?. [online] NATO Review. Available at: http://www.nato.int/docu/Review/2015/Russia/sanctions-after-crimea-have-they-worked/EN/index.htm [Accessed 15 May 2016].

With lower GDP growth rate and country amidst recession, *prima facia,* it could appear that US-EU led sanctions have had a significant impact on Russian economy. However, another key observation could be made by analyzing Russian Stock Exchange (RSX) performance for the period between July 2014 and February 2015. (Figure 15)

Figure 15: Russian Stock Exchange (RSX) performance amidst lower Oil prices (Jul '14 – Feb'15): Comparison of WTI Oil prices return against RSX

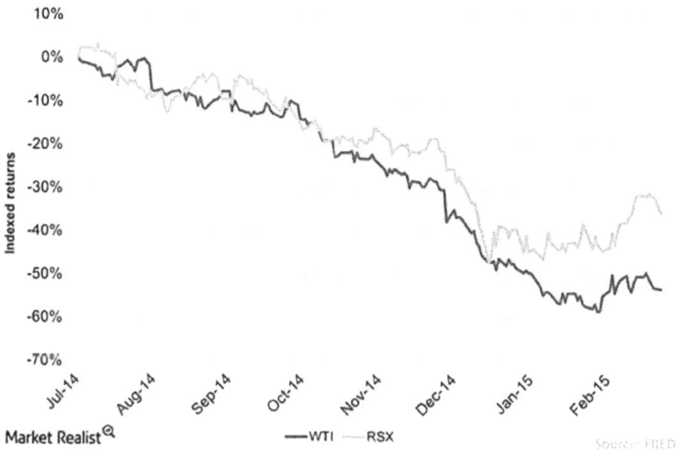

Source: FRED; Russian Stock Exchange

Concluding, major reasons behind downturn in Russian economy from Q3 2014 onward seem to be:

- Overall low prices of its major exports in the international market
- Capital flight, due to earlier recession and economic downturn

Importantly, Russia serves as a major market for European Union. 62% of Russian crude oil reaches EU, and sanctions have had a significant trade effect on EU economies as well.[43] (Figure 16)

Figure 16: Exports of Russian Crude Oil by Destination (FY 2014)

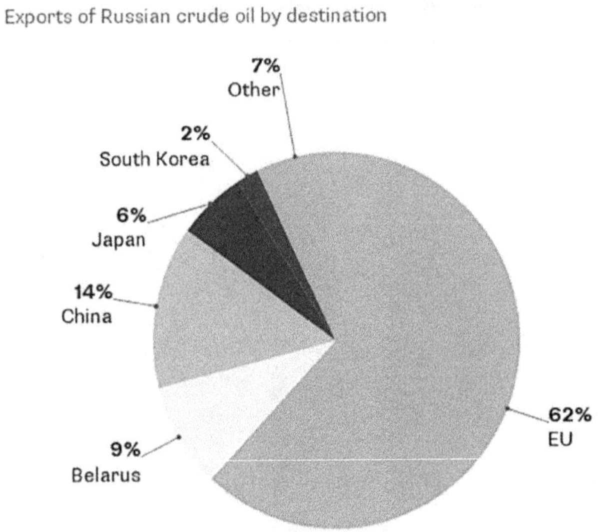

Source: US Energy Information Administration; Bloomberg View

Numerous countries in Europe are dependent on Russian gas. Prime examples of such countries are Poland, Slovakia, Hungary, Latvia, Finland, Lithuania, Estonia, Austria (80% current or planned dependency), and Germany, Italy, and Greece to a varying degree. (Figure 17)

[43] Bershidsky, L. (2015). *Saudi Arabia's Oil War With Russia.* [online] Bloomberg View. Available at: http://www.bloomberg.com/view/articles/2015-10-16/saudi-arabia-s-oil-war-with-russia [Accessed 21 May 2016].

Figure 17: European consumption of Gas supplied by Gazprom

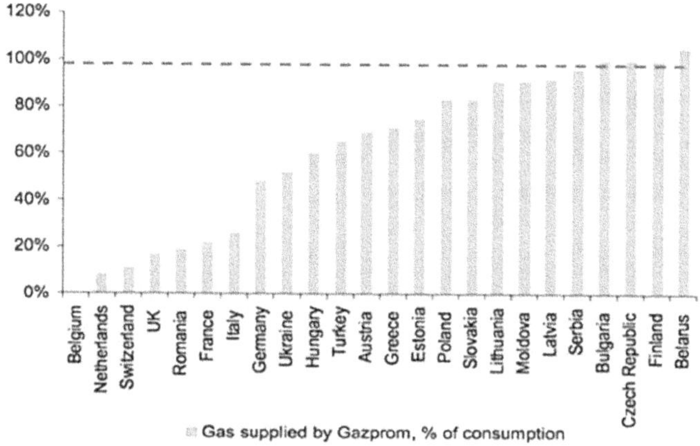

Source: Gazprom; Eurostat (2014)

However, as we observed in aforementioned analyses, the argument that US-EU led sanctions wreak havoc on Russian GDP sounds weak at best.

Latest comments by politicians from Austria, Hungary, Italy, Greece, Germany, and France indicate a possibility of relaxation in geopolitical relations, and an eventual uplifting of sanctions.[44]

It is also noteworthy that Russia has one of the lowest public debt to GDP ratio – around 12% - in the world. Most of its external debt is private. Currently, the country has more than US$ 391.5 Billion in international reserves – 6th highest in the world. This further helped prevent a sovereign debt crisis for the country.

[44] International Business Times. (2016). *EU Unity Crumbles As Russia Sanctions Extension Debate Rages.* [online] Available at: http://www.ibtimes.com/eu-unity-crumbles-russia-sanctions-extension-debate-rages-2376693 [Accessed 4 Jun. 2016].

As of April 2016, inflation rate stands steady at 7.6% year on year growth, while unemployment rate lingers around 5.9%. In January 2016, Bloomberg rated Russia's economy as 12th most innovative in the world.[45]

MICEX – Moscow Interbank Currency Exchange – one of the largest exchange in Russia went up to 8 year high in March 2016. (Figure 18)

Figure 18: MICEX is currently trading at 8-year high

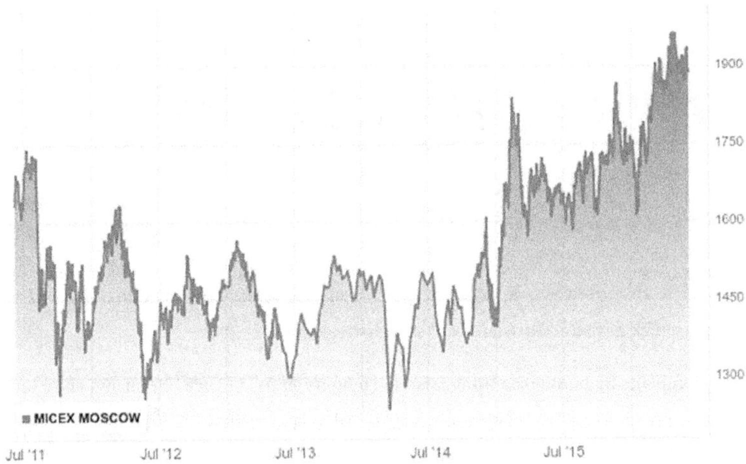

Source: MICEX

Russian government 10Y bond yields soared up around Q4 2014, however are back to pre-sanctions level. (Figure 19)

[45] Bloomberg.com. (2016). *These Are the World's Most Innovative Economies*. [online] Available at: http://www.bloomberg.com/news/articles/2016-01-19/these-are-the-world-s-most-innovative-economies [Accessed 20 May 2016].

Figure 19: Russian Government 10 Y Bond yield back to lowest level of risk in 2 years

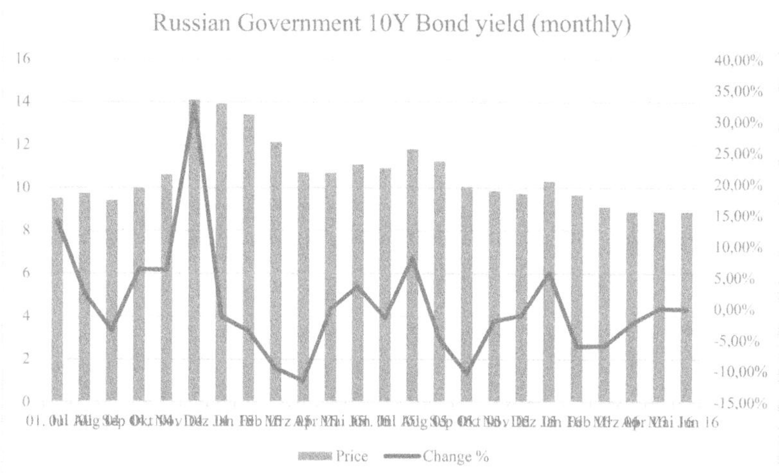

As of 1 June 2016. Source: Investing.com – Russia 10-Year Bond Yield Historical Data

IMF predicts Russian economy to rebound sometime around Q3 2016 or in Q1 of year 2017, with -1.0% growth projection for 2016 and +1% in 2017.[46] Similar forecasts have been projected by World Bank that estimates a -0.7% year-to-year growth for 2016 along with +1.3% GDP growth rate in 2017.[47]

[46] IMF. (2016). World Economic Outlook. [online] Available at: http://www.imf.org/external/pubs/ft/weo/2016/update/01/pdf/0116.pdf [Accessed 17 May 2016].

[47] World Bank. (2015). World Bank Keeps 2015 Growth Projections for Russia, and Slightly Revises 2016-2017 Outlook. [online] Available at: http://www.worldbank.org/en/news/press-release/2015/12/18/world-bank-keeps-2015-growth-projections-for-russia-and-slightly-revises-2016-2017-outlook [Accessed 19 May 2016].

Case study: Islamic Republic of Iran

Understanding impact of sanctions led by the United States, European Union, and United Nations on Islamic Republic of Iran (1979 - present; 2012 – Jan'16; 2006 – Jan'16)

Background

To understand sanctions on Iran and their arguable legitimacy, one must understand the events that led to the first sanctions taking place.

Iran's history is marred by numerous events with their roots and reasons dating back to centuries. For the sake of understanding Iranian history and events surrounding 1979 revolution in particular, Iranian Constitutional Crisis of 1905-07 could be deemed as the beginning point. Traditionally, Iran had a system of monarchy with Shah (King) being the supreme leader. Iranian Constitutional Crisis paved the way for Pahlavi dynasty that replaced earlier monarchy (Qajar). After a brief hiatus, Pahlavi dynasty ruled Iran from 1925 onward, with Reza Shah as the head of monarchy who implemented numerous social reforms in an attempt to transform the country toward a Constitutional monarchy – he attempted to replace Islamic laws with Western ones, forbade separation of sexes, brought about more equality for women and banned niqab.

However, a 1941 Anglo-Soviet invasion replaced him with his son, Mohammad Reza Pahlavi. Although he, like his father, also focused on a swift Westernization/Modernization of the country through so-called White Revolution, it dismayed the traditionalists and working class people. As a result of White Revolution, Iran had, at a time, more than 2200 political prisoners – a number that continued to multiply[48]. General support by the UK, and the US made citizens resentful. Iran witnessed a coup d'état in 1953 led by the UK-US coalition, when the Prime Minister was replaced to further strengthen the hold of

[48] Amnesty. (1978). Amnesty International Report, 1978. [online] Available at: https://www.amnesty.org/download/Documents/204000/pol100011978eng.pdf [Accessed 19 May 2016].

Mohammad Reza Pahlavi, and to privatize the Iranian oil under foreign-owned companies.[49]

Religious Shia cleric, Ayatollah Khomeini, rose to the prominence during 1963 voicing public dissatisfaction against the Shah and White Revolution; he was arrested, and was exiled for 15 years out of the country. 1970s saw an Oil boom, with rising revenue came the divide between the rich and the poor, and more unrest. Disregard for traditions, increasing disparity, censorship, police brutality – all these formed as major factors for an event that changed the course of Iran's history.

Ayatollah Khomeini later on moved to France, where he gave sermons to incentivize people to protest against the government. Suddenly he found a backing of the French and the British – who had now withdrawn their support for the Shah. Eventually, Iran saw massive, radicalized protests throughout the country, and witnessed the establishment of Islamic Republic government. [50] Secularists were swept away from the country, and Iran found itself as a radicalized, Islamic republic.

Amidst this, Iran hostage crisis took place. Angered and disgruntled group of revolutionaries captured the American Embassy in Tehran and kept its staff hostage for 444 days. (November 1979 - January 1981) Western media portrayed the events as act of vengeance, anarchy, and terrorism; Iran saw it as a blow against the United States and its interference in the domestic matters, and against its support for the autocratic Shah.[51] This led to the first sanctions imposed by the United States on Iran.

[49] Bryne, M. (2013). *CIA Admits It Was Behind Iran's Coup.* [online] Foreign Policy. Available at: http://foreignpolicy.com/2013/08/19/cia-admits-it-was-behind-irans-coup/ [Accessed 19 May 2016].
[50] YouTube. (2016). *Imam Khomeini - The Man Who Changed The World | Iran & The West [Part 1/3].* [online] Available at: https://www.youtube.com/watch?v=FfrJ2rBobGs [Accessed 9 May 2016].
[51] Historyguy.com. (2016). *The History Guy: Iran-U.S. Hostage Crisis (1979-1981).* [online] Available at: http://www.historyguy.com/iran-us_hostage_crisis.html [Accessed 23 May 2016].

EU-UN led sanctions: Background

Right at the time when Khomeini came to power, Iranian revolution had just taken place, and the Iranian hostage crisis was still on, Iraq – under the leadership of Saddam Hussein – invaded Iran in September 1980.

Iraq-Iran war lasted for over 8 years, and ended in a stalemate. Already weakened by Iranian Revolution in 1979, the war significantly weakened the economy of Iran. However, it also awakened a nationalist tendency among the populace, with Iran coming out as even more united, and radicalized country than a decade back. To escalate the events further, US passively supported Iraq, and in 1988, shot down a civil airline, Iran Air Flight 655 – killing 290 passengers and crew.[52]

Coming out of the above-mentioned events, Iran was determined to further strengthen its position, against both the West and the rival Arab countries.

Following 1979 Revolution and amid an armed conflict against Iraq, Iran decide to revive its Nuclear program, which– quite ironically –began with the support of the United States in 1950s in the first place.[53] In 1980s, Iran entered into negotiations with France and Argentina – who later refunded or cancelled the agreements - and eventually, gained the support of Russia in the 90s forming a joint research organization.

International Atomic Energy Agency (IAEA) reported in 2003 that Iran failed to disclose sensitive enrichment and reprocessing activities that it was obliged to under NPT (Non-Proliferation Treaty), although it reported no evidence of links to a nuclear weapons program.[54] Iran refused to give up its enrichment program, arguing for a need for its energy security, along with the fact that cancelling the program deprives it from its inalienable rights to peaceful nuclear technology. Eventual tensions in 2000s on nuclear program led to the UN sanctions (Resolution 1737) in 2006, and subsequent EU sanctions in 2012.

[52] Fisk, R. (2004). *The Great War for civilization.* London: Fourth Estate.
[53] Roe, S. (2007). *An atomic threat made in America.* [online] chicagotribune.com. Available at: http://www.chicagotribune.com/news/nationworld/chi-061209atoms-day1-story,0,2034260.htmlstory [Accessed 18 May 2016].
[54] IAEA. (2003). *IAEA GOV/2003/40: Implementation of the NPT safeguards agreement in the Islamic Republic of Iran.* [online] Available at: http://www.iaea.org/Publications/Documents/Board/2003/gov2003-40.pdf [Accessed 20 May 2016].

Aftermath and impact

For the brevity of our analysis and for a more coherent understand of how sanctions have affected Iran's economy, we shall primarily focus on period post-UN sanctions, however taking US led sanctions into account. It is difficult to fully analyze and comprehend the impact on Iranian economy because of US sanctions; United States imposed first sanctions in 1979 however gradually increased it in 1990s. Furthermore, Iran experienced a significant destruction of its economy in the 80s due to the Iraq-Iran war; 90s saw second Gulf War along with Asian financial crisis that severely affected its major trade partners.

In the midst of a region marred with both oil (economic) and geopolitical wars, Iran's decision to initiate and continue their nuclear and ballistic missile programs resulted in significant trade sanctions against them. Between 2006 to 2010, United Nations Security Council passed 6 resolutions targeting Iran's nuclear and missile programs. While these resolutions were punitive, they eventually led to sanctions that were more significant in nature by the European Union – at time, one of the biggest trading partners of Iran.[55]

In the following pages, we shall observe at how Iran's export crumbled as sanctions imposed by (US-), United Nations, and European Union grew harsher. Furthermore, we shall also try to count in any other factors that might come into play and could have impact into the numbers, along with looking at major macroeconomic indicators.

[55] Samore, G. (2015). *Sanctions Against Iran: A Guide to Targets, Terms, and Timetables.* [online] Harvard Kennedy School. Available at: http://belfercenter.ksg.harvard.edu/files/Iran%20Sanctions.pdf [Accessed 18 May 2016].

The Oil Economy

Crude Oil and Natural Gas – these are the two lifelines of Iran's export-oriented economy. As of 2014, more than US$39.5 Billion worth of Iranian exports consisted of mineral fuels, oils, waxes etc. In other words, 77% of total exports (US$ 53.6 Billion) constitute of aforementioned products. (Figure 20)

Figure 20: Iranian exports in 2014

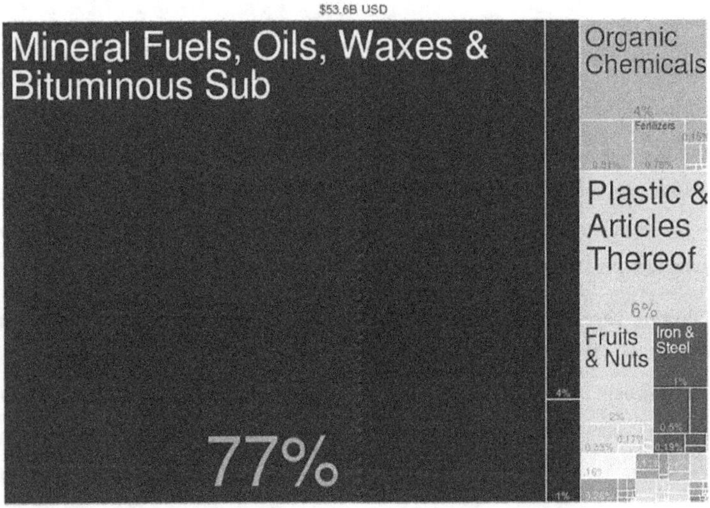

Source: The Atlas of Economic Complexity, Center for Economic Development, Harvard University

Islamic Republic of Iran possess around 10% of the world's proven oil reserves, and 15% of total global gas reserves.[56] Despite destruction of several oil-processing facilities during the First Gulf War, Iran continues to be a leading producer of oil and natural gas, and particularly expanded its capacity between 2007 and 2012.[57]

[56] Eia.doe.gov. (2016). *Iran - U.S. Energy Information Administration (EIA)*. [online] Available at: http://www.eia.doe.gov/countries/cab.cfm?fips=IR [Accessed 19 May 2016].
[57] Schweid, B. (2008). *Iran Oil industry founders*. [online] Seattle Times. Available at: http://seattletimes.nwsource.com/html/nationworld/2003494872_iranoil26.html [Accessed 19 May 2016].

Before sanctions, European Union used to be one of the prime markets for Iranian crude exports. In 2008, Iranian exports to the EU stood at US$ 14 Billion; despite punitive sanctions imposed by the UN and exhaustive measures in place, in 2011, Iran was the 7th largest crude oil exporter to the European Union.[58] (Figure 21)

Figure 21: European Oil Export Market Share before sanctions

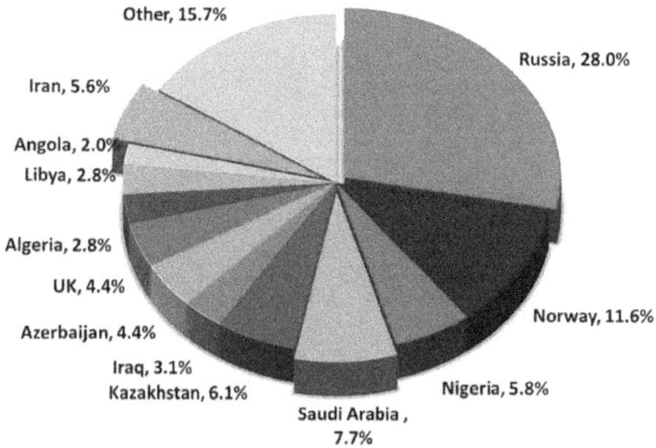

Source: Katusa Research (2016)

However, this completely changed with the introduction of European sanctions on Iran. (Figure 22) Within 3 years after escalation of UN-led sanctions, Iran's market share at 5.6% was completely nullified, and taken over by other leading crude oil exporting countries.

[58] Ec.europa.eu. (2016). *Iran - Trade - European Commission*. [online] Available at: http://ec.europa.eu/trade/creating-opportunities/bilateral-relations/countries/iran/ [Accessed 19 May 2016].

Figure 22: European Market Share of Top Crude Exporters

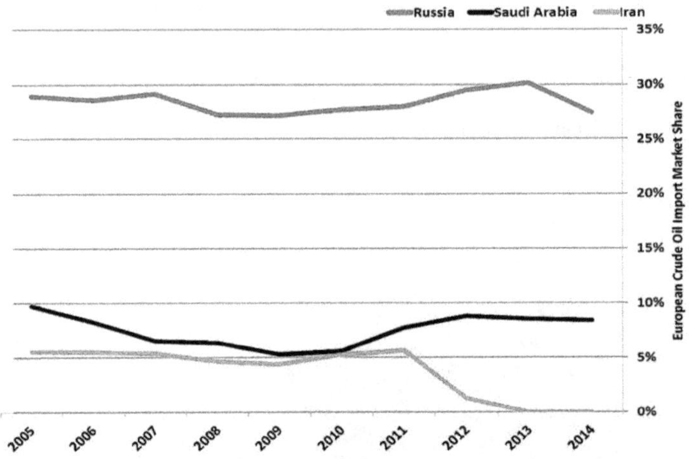

Source: Katusa Research (2016)

Iran was the leading crude oil exporting country to European Union until eve of 2012, when the sanctions were dropped. Sanctions imposed by European Union, and significant expansion of sanctions by the United Nations in 2012 meant that the country had not only lost its major market, it was not also difficult for it to access markets in other countries.

An interim agreement took place in November 2013, called Geneva interim agreement (officially, Joint Plan of Action) between Iran, and China, France, the United Kingdom, Russian Federation, and the United States (collectively known as P5+1). Iranian position, so far, had been that it had the right to enrich uranium, whereas the US and Germany-UK-France maintained that the nuclear program of Iran possesses a significant risk to the international community and failed to meet international obligations outlined under NPT.

The agreements ended without reaching a conclusion, and later posed a significant damage to Iranian economy. Nonetheless, eventually the Geneva agreement led to final negotiations, leading to cancellation of UN-EU sanctions in January 2016.

Figure 23: Iranian Crude Oil Exports: Pre- and Post- interim agreement

Buyer	Average Pre-sanctions (2011)	Average Post-interim Agreement (2014 -)	Percent change
European Union	600,000	Negligible	-100%
China	550,000	410,000	-25%
Japan	325,000	190,000	-40%
India	320,000	190,000	-40%
South Korea	230,000	130,000	-40%
South Africa	80,000	0	-100%
Malaysia	55,000	0	-100%
Sri Lanka	35,000	Negligible	-100%
Taiwan	35,000	10,000	-70%
Singapore	20,000	0	-100%
Other countries	55,000	Negligible	-100%
Total	**2.505 Million**	**1.057 Million**	**-60%**

Measured in barrels/day. Source: International Energy Agency; Congressional Research Service

Between 2011 and period lingering around mid-2014, Iran experienced a complete trade reduction in its traditional markets – EU, China, and India. Latter two countries remained an exception, with far more alliance with Iranian economy, however political and economic implications of both UN and EU sanctions laid pressure on several other countries to severe or reduce economic ties with Iran. (Figure 23)

Economic Growth amidst sanctions

Iranian economy for year 2005-6 was marked by a significant growth, thanks to rising oil prices in the market, and reduction in regional and global geopolitical issues. In fact, even during global financial crisis of 2008-9, Iran was one of the very few countries that not only survived the economic recession, but also came out well ahead of it. (Figure 24) This could be partly explained by demand, and search for unconventional trade partners among other nations.

Figure 24: Iran: Annual GDP growth rate (2005 – 2014)

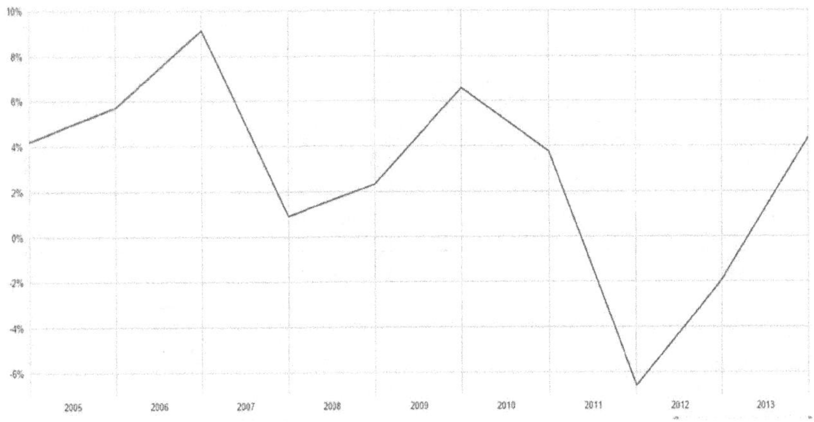

Source: World Bank

Between 2002 and 2006, inflation rate in Iran hovered around 14%.[59] Around 2008, more than 55% of the revenue came from oil and natural gas; it is noteworthy that the Iranian government gives out significant cash handouts and subsidies, and there is little alignment between its fiscal and monetary policy. Most of the country works in shadow economy, and the budget in itself is highly dependent on the price of oil; these factors contributed to both fall and rise in GDP growth rate of Iran in past decade.

[59] Indexmundi.com. (2010). *Iran Inflation rate (consumer prices) - Economy*. [online] Available at: http://www.indexmundi.com/iran/inflation_rate_(consumer_prices).html [Accessed 17 May 2016].

Currency fluctuations

Amidst most recent sanctions that were placed by European Union, Iran's currency, Iranian Real (IRR), lost a significant value and was devalued in July 2013.[60] Iranian Economic Reform Plan actively advocates redenomination since 1980s; this could be further observed by the fact that June 2013, USDIRR traded at around US$ 1 = 12,093. As of June 2016, it trades at US$ 1 = 30,048, due to a further devaluation in July '13 (Figure 25)

Figure 25: USDIRR exchange rate between Jan'08 - Jan'16

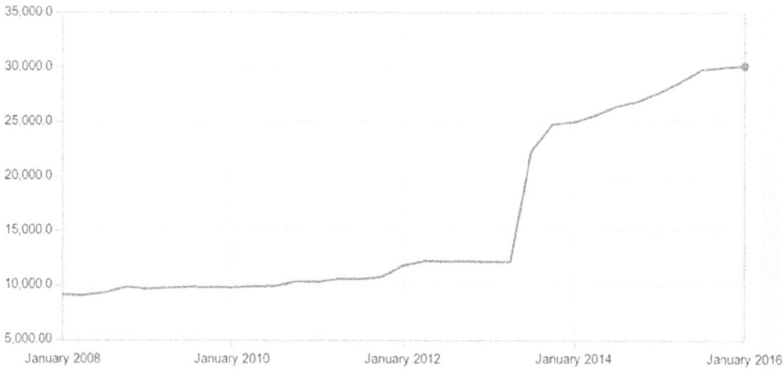

Source: OANDA, Historical Rates USDIRR

Inflation remains a huge problem; between 2011-2015, inflation rate hovered around 12 to 16% per annum.[61] Unemployment rate also piqued at 12%, however finding clear and reliable numbers remains a challenge; opposition government sources estimate unemployment rate to be up to 22-30%.[62]

[60] Cia.gov. (2016). *The World Factbook.* [online] Available at: https://www.cia.gov/library/publications/the-world-factbook/geos/ir.html [Accessed 19 May 2016].

[61] France24. (2015). *Iran Five Year Plan targets annual 8% growth.* [online] Available at: http://www.france24.com/en/20100111-iran-five-year-plan-targets-annual-8-growth?quicktabs_1=0 [Accessed 19 May 2016].

[62] latimes. (2012). *Prices in Iran rise after lifting of subsidies.* [online] Available at: http://www.latimes.com/news/nationworld/world/la-fg-iran-subsidies-20101223,0,5543095.story?track=rss [Accessed 19 May 2016].

Conclusion

After years of discussions, United Nations and European Union deescalated the situation, came to the agreement with Iranian government, and UN removed sanctions against Iran in January 16, 2016. (US sanctions remain in place, however loosened up to a certain degree)

They come at the same time when crude oil prices – the most important export for Iran - are one of the lowest in recent times. Iran is an energy superpower.[63] (Figure 26 and Figure 27)

Figure 26: Countries with the largest oil reserves in the world

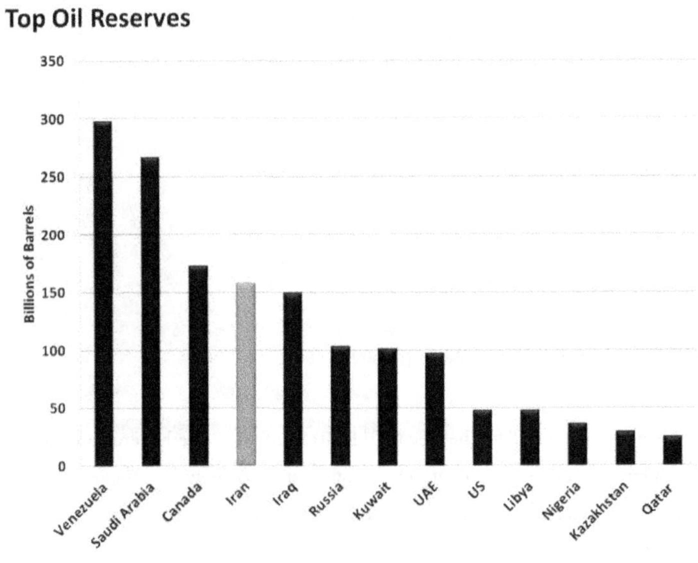

Source: Katusa Research (2016)

[63] Google Books. (2014). *Energy and the Iranian economy : hearing*. [online] Available at: https://books.google.com/books?id=CA1Cn8tDMv4C&pg=PA50&dq=iran+energy+superpower&hl=en&sa=X&ei=uBKYU6jJOabLsQT9y4DIDQ&ved=0CC0Q6AEwAw#v=onepage&q=energy%20superpower&f=false [Accessed 19 May 2016].

Figure 27: Countries with the largest gas reserves in the world

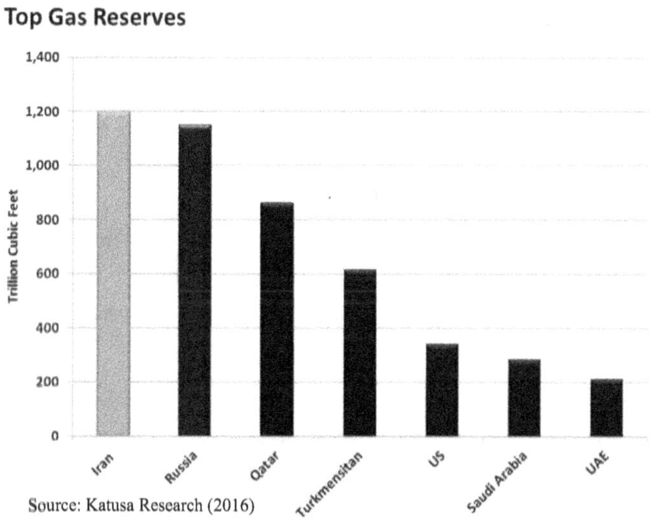

Source: Katusa Research (2016)

Wall Street Journal reports that Iranian natural gas could start to play a significant part of the European Union's energy mix after next 3 to 4 years; European Commission itself estimates that EU could be importing up to 25 to 35 Billion cubic meters of gas from Iran in coming years.[64] Other countries such as India has also expressed an interest in setting up an LNG terminal in Chahabar port in Iran.

Days after sanctions were lifted off of Iran, Saudi Arabian stocks fell 5.4%, Kuwait and Qatar stock exchanges experienced 3.1% and 4.6% drop, respectively, while stocks in Qatar saw an enormous 7% decline – these were one of the lowest levels in almost 7 years for the aforementioned countries.[65]

---

[64] Seekingalpha.com. (2016). *Iranian Sanctions Repealed - Focus On Natural Gas.* [online] Available at: http://seekingalpha.com/article/3977759-iranian-sanctions-repealed-focus-natural-gas [Accessed 19 May 2016].

[65] Seekingalpha.com. (2016). *Middle East Stocks Crash On Iran Sanctions: ETFs To Watch.* [online] Available at: http://seekingalpha.com/article/3826376-middle-east-stocks-crash-iran-sanctions-etfs-watch [Accessed 26 May 2016].

Case study: Republic of Cuba

Impact of United States embargo on Republic of Cuba (October 1960 – present)

Background

For more than 50 years, United States has unilaterally imposed an economic and financial embargo against Cuba. For more than 22 years continuously, United Nations has passed a resolution condemning the embargo; in the latest resolution, more than 180 countries supported the resolution with 2 against (United States and Israel). [66] However, what is the reason for this embargo that lasts for more than half a century already?

In 1898, Cuba fought its last war of independence against Spanish colonialists. It was one of three liberation wars that Cuba had fought against Spain in 19th century, and Maximo Gomez emerged as the leader for Cuban independence struggle. Manifesto of Montecristi – as it was known at the time – was the announcement of war, signed in 1894, and outlined the policy for Cuba's war for independence.

In the final 3 months, the conflict escalated into Spanish-American war, with United States fighting against Kingdom of Spain in the Philippines, Puerto Rico, and Cuba. Apart from immense financial investments and interests of Cuban emigres, the Spanish-American War was also fueled by immense propaganda and yellow journalism.

Outcome of the war resulted in a US American victory over Kingdom of Spain, with both countries signing the Treaty of Paris in December 1898, resulting in Cuban independence.

General of the Cuban War of Independence, Gerard Machado, became the first President of Cuba in 1925. He leaped into a massive modernization plan for the country, with a determination to make Cuba, 'Switzerland of the Americas.' Re-elected for another term, his idealism did not last long and Machado became more autocratic, and amended constitution in order to seek a further, third election. He was soon overthrown in a

[66] Reuters. (2014). *For 23rd time, U.N. nations urge end to U.S. embargo on Cuba.* [online] Available at: http://www.reuters.com/article/2014/10/28/us-cuba-un-idUSKBN0IH1RN20141028 [Accessed 25 May 2016].

bloodless coup, orchestrated by the US Ambassador and Cuban War of Independence veterans.[67]

Through this coup, Fulegencio Batista rose to the power. He instated the 1940 Cuban Constitution, and served one presidency term from 1940-44. After a while, he moved to the United States, only to return in 1952 and re-run for presidency. Facing electoral defeat though, Batista launched a military coup, suspended 1940 Constitution, tightened media censorship, and revoked most political liberties. Furthermore, he aligned himself with major sugar-plantation owners, and negotiated relationships for American mafia in drug, gambling, and prostitution business with US-based multinationals. [68] Batista also utilized his Bureau for the Repression of Communist Activities (Buró de Represión de Actividades Comunistas), to carry out violence, torture, public executions – resulting in death of anywhere between 1,000 to 20,000 people. Until 1959, Batista and his government received financial, logistical, and military support of the United States.[69]

Beginning July 26, 1953, Fidel Castro orchestrated a revolutionary organization to overthrow Batista, aptly named – the 26th of July movement. Batista was completely backed by the United States; however, 26th of July movement fought his dictatorship on both rural and urban fronts. Eventually, Batista was defeated in the Battle of Santa Clara by rebels under the command of Che Guevera in January 1, 1959. He soon fled to the United States.

Cuba came under the role of a new government with new leaders – it became a revolutionary socialist state, with communist government, and Fidel Castro as their leader. To begin with, role and massive support of the United States to a dictator did not help in normalization of situation and completely changed the US-Cuban relationship. However, United States canceled the decision to import 700,000 tons of sugar from Cuba, and refused oil export to the country; for a country that was urgently in need of oil and gas, and relied on sugar exports as its main revenue, this was a massive setback. Cuba was dependent on

[67] DUR, P. and GILCREASE, C. (2002). US Diplomacy and the Downfall of a Cuban Dictator: Machado in 1933. *Journal of Latin American Studies*, [online] 34(02), pp.255-282. Available at: http://dx.doi.org/10.1017/S0022216X02006417 [Accessed 24 May 2016].
[68] Olson, J. (2000). *Historical dictionary of the 1950s*. Westport, Conn.: Greenwood Press.
[69] Grandin, G. and Joseph, G. (2010). *A century of revolution*. Durham [NC]: Duke University Press.

Soviet crude oil halfway across the world; it nationalized the oil-refineries owned by US Americans in the country.

End result: United States decided to put a complete commercial, economic, and financial embargo on Cuba beginning October 1960. [70] The aim of the sanctions is to maintain them so long as the Cuban government refuses to move toward 'democratization and greater respect for human rights.'[71]

US embargo is based on following statutes and regulations:

- Trading With the Enemy Act of 1917, section 5(b);
- Foreign Assistance Act of 1961, section 620(a);
- Cuba Assets Control Regulations of 1963;
- Cuban Democracy Act of 1992;
- Cuban Liberty and Democratic Solidarity (Libertad) Act of 1996, (Helms-Burton Act);
- The Trade Sanctions Reform and Export Enhancement Act of 2000

Warming of Cuba-United States relations began in December 2014. Known as Cuban thaw, it resulted in diplomatic relations being reestablished after more than 54 years. US sanctions, however, continue to this day.[72]

[70] Archives.chicagotribune.com. (1960). *Ike Slashes Sugar Quotas*. [online] Available at: http://archives.chicagotribune.com/1960/07/07/page/1/article/ike-slashes-cuban-sugar-quota [Accessed 30 May 2016].
[71] State.gov. (1992). *Cuba Democracy Act*. [online] Available at: http://www.state.gov/www/regions/wha/cuba/democ_act_1945.html [Accessed 23 May 2016].
[72] Aljazeera.com. (2015). *US and Cuba restore ties by opening embassies*. [online] Available at: http://www.aljazeera.com/news/2015/07/cuba-restore-ties-opening-embassies-150720024721778.html [Accessed 25 May 2016].

Impact

Impact of US embargo on Republic of Cuba is hard to assess, primarily because:

- Prior to embargo, Cuba itself was marred with a civil conflict resulting in destruction of a properly functional economy;
- Cuba switched to a socialist, communist-style government with centrally planned economy, which makes it hard to differentiate between whether any macroeconomic changes were a result of embargo or socialist policies etc.;
- More importantly, despite US pressure, Cuba could and did establish trade ties with rest of the world. Thus, United States is the only country in the world which does not have normalized trade relations with the country.

Interestingly – or ironically –, United States is the 5th largest exporter to Cuba, accounting for Cuba's 6.6% imports.[73] Cuba pays for all the products in cash, and credit is not allowed for any trade between the two countries.

Confiscated wealth in 1960s helped improve living standards for millions of Cubans through education, land distribution, and allocated apartments. In 1959, these assets were worth more than US$ 9 Billion. Citizens did not pay any personal income tax, and Cuba even provided significant foreign aid to other countries. Very generous subsidies and support from the Soviet Union helped Cuba progress further and maintain these standards; however, when Soviet Union crumbled, so did Cuba. This was known as the 'Special period' (Período especial) in Cuba.[74]

With collapse of the USSR, Cuba's GDP declined by 35% between 1989 and 1993 due to the loss of more than 80% of its trading partners and subsidies from the Soviet Union.[75] This came right at the time when global prices for sugar crashed completely.

---

[73] Cia.gov. (2012). *The World Factbook.* [online] Available at: https://www.cia.gov/library/publications/the-world-factbook/geos/cu.html [Accessed 22 May 2016].
[74] Zerohedge.com. (2016). *Cuba – A History | Zero Hedge.* [online] Available at: http://www.zerohedge.com/contributed/2014-05-06/cuba-%E2%80%93-history [Accessed 24 May 2016].
[75] Pike, J. (2015). *Cuba's Economy.* [online] Globalsecurity.org. Available at: http://www.globalsecurity.org/military/world/cuba/economy.htm [Accessed 25 May 2016].

Figure 28: Cuban exports in 2014

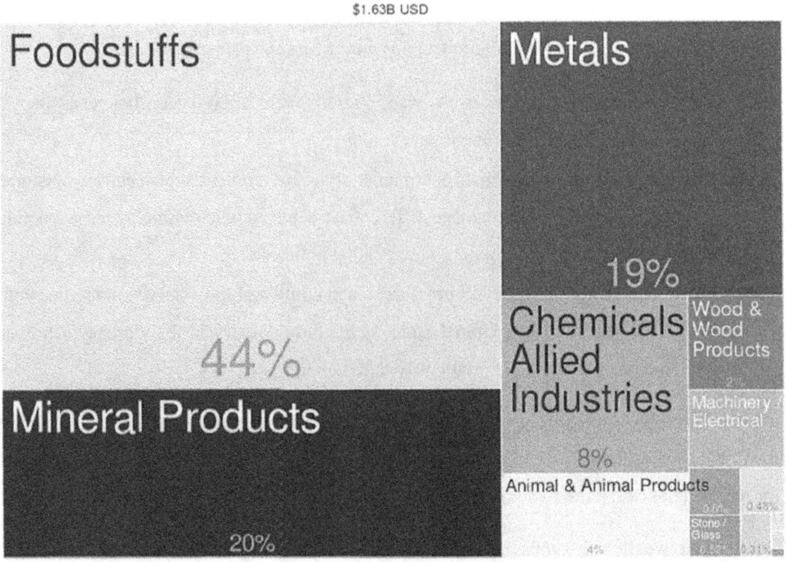

Source: The Atlas of Economic Complexity, Center for International Development, Harvard University

More than 44% of Cuba's exports comprise of foodstuffs: sugars and confectionary, beverages, spirits, and vinegar, and tobacco, and tobacco substances along with renowned Cuban cigars. Sugars and confectionary alone make up for ~ 21% of total exports, at US$ 348 Million. Total exports in 2014 were US$ 1.63 Billion. (Figure 28)

When it comes to actual analysis and understanding of the impact of US trade embargo, we run into an issue where the period of embargo started much earlier, and at the time when Cuba was going through a socio-political and economic turmoil and transition. Another key difference is that Cuba is one of the very few major examples in terms of sanctions placed unilaterally by one country on another, for such an extended period of time.

In fact, it can very well be argued that the collapse of Soviet Union had far bigger impact on Cuban economy than any other single factor. (Figure 29)

Figure 29: Cuba GDP growth between 1971 and 2013

Source: World Bank

In 1988, 85% of Cuba's trade was with Soviet bloc; by 1992, these levels were lingering around 26%. On the other hand, Cuba represented less than 5% of total US exports and imports before 1960s, and this level was arguably on such a level that it did not turn into a drastic risk for Cuba.

One of the most comprehensive studies on impact of US embargo on Cuba was conducted by ITC using a gravity model. Primarily, the trade data from 1996-98 was estimated for quantitative impact of sanctions on bilateral trade and investments, and postulating econometric models.

Based on the aforementioned study, estimates for loss of Cuban imports are somewhere between 17-27%, this averages around US$ 658 Million to US$ 1 Billion. Using the same trade data, ITC estimated that US imports from Cuba would be somewhere around US$ 69 Million – US$ 149 Million per year, or approximately 7-15% of total Cuban exports.[76]

[76] Teegen, H. (n.d.). *Economic and Strategic Impacts of US Economic sanctions on Cuba.* [online] George Washington University. Available at: https://www.gwu.edu/~clai/working_papers/Teegen_Hildy_02-03.pdf [Accessed 25 May 2016].

Nonetheless, it could be very well argued that both the countries have divulged and divested in trade relations with other countries. (Figure 30)

Figure 30: Cuba's global export share between 2000-2014

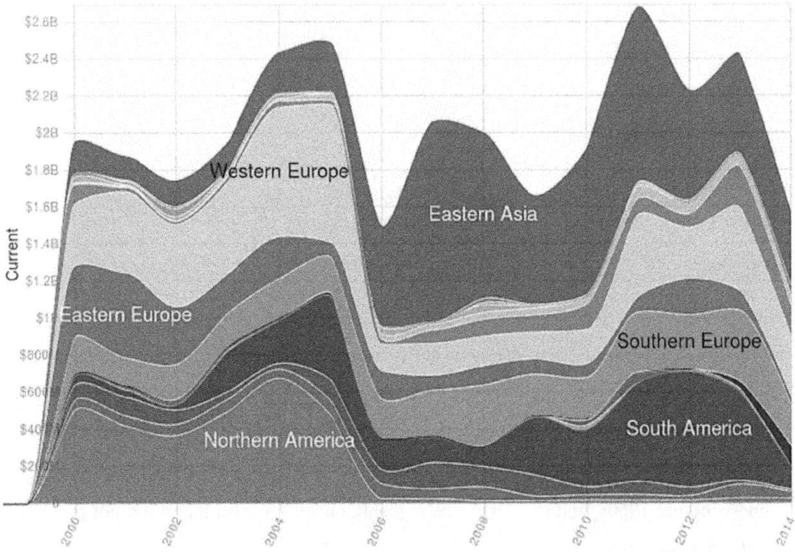

Source: The Atlas of Economic Complexity, Center for International Development, Harvard University

China has recently emerged as one of the largest trade partners of Cuba, accounting for more than 20% of all its exports. It is followed by the Spain, United Kingdom, Germany, Brazil, and Canada and is behind Venezuela.

Current scenario

Despite US embargo, in numerous statistics, Cuba punches well above its weight. Its GDP PPP, it has considerably higher income per capita than Mexico and several other Latin American countries. Debt as the percentage of GDP is 35.3%, and it invests far more in foreign countries than most equivalent countries with similar economy and/or population.

It also has an established public infrastructure network, particularly, railway network; and its Human Development Index constantly ranks ahead of most of the other countries in the Caribbean and Latin America. Inflation estimates for 2015 remained at 4.4%, and GDP growth projection is 4.7%, along with a low unemployment rate of 3%.[77] While not always reliable, most scrutinized publicly available numbers from the government indicate a poverty level that is one of the lowest in developing world – around 4th in Latin America.

Recent thaw in the relations leads us to a scenario where Cuba could have access to more markets, and in particular, more tourism from the United States. A way to analyze impact of embargo, or reopening of trade relations if to look from different perspective, bring us to a report that puts the number in ballpark of US $ 43 Billion in total economic impact.[78]

However, Cuba's GDP per capita is still around the same figure as it was in 1985; it has been below demographic replacement age since 1978, and as the population is shrinking and ageing, this could result in huge issues for the country in the future.

[77] Reuters. (2016). *Cuba economic growth rises to 4.7 pct in first half -minister*. [online] Available at: http://www.reuters.com/article/2015/07/15/cuba-economy-idUSL2N0ZV1PR20150715 [Accessed 19 May 2016].
[78] Texas A&M University. (2016). *Emerging Markets for U.S. Agriculture: Focus on Cuba*. [online] Available at: http://cnas.tamu.edu/Publications/E312.pdf [Accessed 30 May 2016].

Conclusion

As witnessed in the case of Russia, Iran, and Cuba, international economic sanction do not seem to have a significant impact on the target country's economy.

Russia experienced a significant economic downturn in Q3 2014, which coincided with both sanctions and falling oil prices. However, as we have shown earlier, the downturn can be primarily attributed to the fall in global commodity prices for its biggest export product, i.e. oil and natural gas, with sanction being a secondary or insignificant factor per se. It also successfully negotiated and further developed trade relations with other countries, especially in Asia, that emerged as new market for its export commodity. Russian economy is expected to have a rebound in FY 2017-18, as the IMF and World Bank predict as well.

Iran seemed to have no significant bearing from the sanctions imposed by the United States, however, it did experience a significant economic shock and an eventual downturn after the sanctions were laid down by the United Nations. Further sanctions by the European Union – at time its one of the biggest trading partners -, further deteriorated the economic state of the country, with a mild rebound coming from alliances with other trading partners.

Cuba, on the other hand, is an overtly complicated country to fully assess and analyze the impact of US embargo. Most of the analyses, macroeconomic indicators, and other cited work have equally showed that while country does not seem to have a significant disadvantage due to the US trade embargo in itself, an eventual restoration in trade relations could be immensely helpful for Cuban economy.

Arguments for effectiveness of sanctions

Primarily research that sanctions can achieve their foreign policy goals was conducted by Gary Hufbauer et al, published in 1985 and later updated in 1990. Their findings focused on sanctions between 1914 to 1990, focusing on more than 115 cases, and concluded that more than 34%, or 40 cases, showed that sanctions were successful in attaining their intended objectives.[79] Hugbauer et al found that in more than 52% of the instances, sanctions work to destabilize the country, whereas in 33% of the cases, they may modestly influence the policy changes or check on the military adventures of the target country.

In particular, it could be observed in Iran's case – although assessing it completely would be virtually impossible owing to the fact that Iran faced issues on three fronts: sanctions, war, and domestic revolution; the US sanctions do not appear to have had a significant impact on the economy. Ideological regimes can have a high 'pain' threshold for their populace, and despite a poorly managed economy and structural weakness, Iran experienced a significant impact on economy primarily due to the UN-led sanctions.

Matthias Neuenkirch and Florian Neumeier argued through an empirical research that imposition of sanctions highly depends on the imposing party, timeline, and the target country. US-led sanctions seemed to decrease GDP growth in the target state by 0.5% to 0.9% over 7 years. UN-led sanctions, on the other hand, have a wider and much harsher effect; they seem to decrease real GDP growth in the target state by 2.3% to 3.5%. and their adverse effects could last for up to a decade.[80]

Survey: Domestic perception on effect of sanctions

Numbers can be misleading, misconstrued, misrepresented. Often, it is essential to understand the perception of people living in the target country – in particular, how they gauge the effect of the sanctions on the country. For this, we carried out an anonymous poll on a public internet forum, and asked the respondents questions such as:

[79] Hufbauer, G. (2007). *Economic sanctions reconsidered.* Washington, DC: Peterson Institute for International Economics.
[80] Neuenkirch, M. and Neumeier, F. (2014). *The Impact of UN and US Economic Sanctions on GDP Growth.* [online] Marburg Centre for Institutional Economics •. Available at: https://www.uni-marburg.de/fb02/macie/research/output/macie/neuenkirch_neumeier_2014_2.pdf [Accessed 8 Jun. 2016].

1. How would you describe current economic situation in the country? (Available answer choices: Bad, Good/Not bad, and Don't know)
2. Who is responsible for issues with current economic situation in the country? (Available answer choices: West (US/EU/et cetera), Government (Domestic government), and Oil prices and other factors)
3. How noticeable do you find impact of sanctions on day-to-day life? (Available answer choices: Noticeable; Not noticeable)

In particular, sample size for Iran was too small (<9 respondents), and survey for Cuba also offered similar challenges. Nonetheless, we carried out a survey asking respondents from Russia, and their views on sanctions with the aforementioned questions. Although the poll was anonymous, to ensure credibility, the language of the survey was Russian, and only the answers from respondents with Russian IP addresses were taken into consideration.

Information, underlying assumptions, and shortcomings of the survey:

Sample size for this survey constituted 56 respondents. While this is not a massive sample size, nonetheless it was enough for us to draw conclusive arguments further validating our findings. However, the shortcomings of the survey could be:

1. Underlying assumption: Posted in Russian language, gathers answers from Russian IP address. Nonetheless, this could not rule out the possibility of (Russian speaking-) expatriates living in Russia may also answer.
2. Posted on a social media forum: Possible demography of such social media forum indicate – English-speaking, internet-savvy, young participants, hailing from big cities. (1 million+)

Figure 31: Perception on current economic situation in the country

Sample size: 56 respondents; survey included answers only in Russian language and from Russian IP address to ensure better credibility; includes answers collected within 24 hours of publishing the survey; posted on an internet forum in Russian language primarily

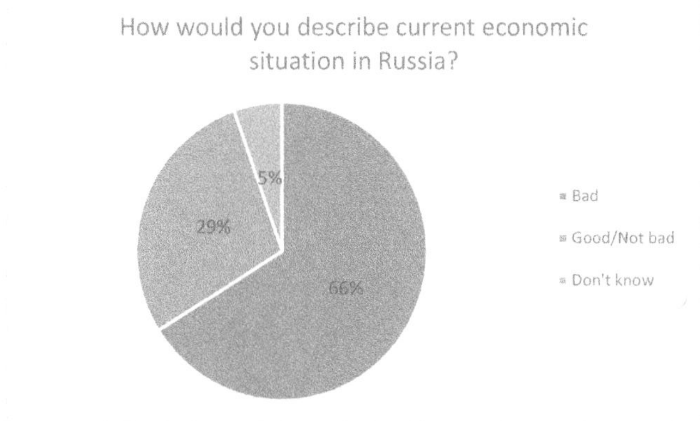

Question 1: How would you describe current economic situation in Russia?

Out of 56 respondents, nearly 66% (37 respondents) answered that the current economic situation is 'bad' in Russia. It comes as unsurprising given the macroeconomic indicators that depict the state of the country's economy, nonetheless, 29%, or 16 respondents, said that the current economic situation is either 'good' or 'not bad'. (Figure 31)

This further alludes to the argument made earlier that the current economy in Russia, although bad in shape, is slowly recovering. In addition, the impact of the sanction could possibly be limited to few industries or few areas in life for general population.

Figure 32: Domestic perception on responsibility for current economic woes

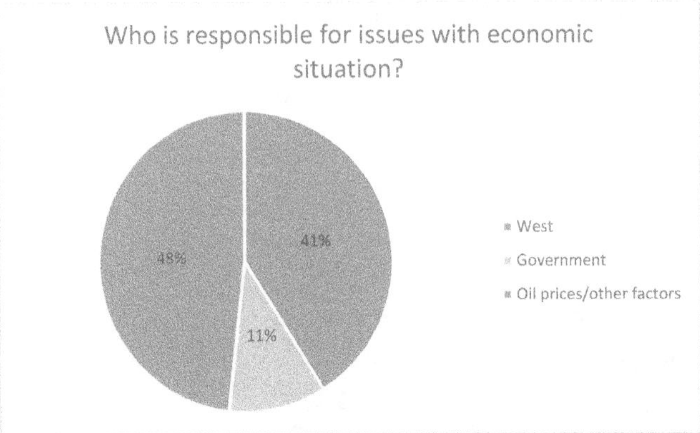

Question 2: Who is responsible for issues with economic situation?

Nearly half (48%), or 27 respondents, believe that oil prices and/or other factors are responsible for issues with current economy in the country. This is in line with our findings; nonetheless, it could also be interpreted that domestic leaders make sure to attribute the reasons for economic downturn on external factors. 41% respondents (23), for instance, argue that 'West', comprising of the US, EU etc. is the reason for issue that Russian economy is facing, whereas only 11%, or 6 respondents, find Russian government to be the primary reason behind economic woes in the country. (Figure 32)

Figure 33: Effect of sanctions on day-to-day life

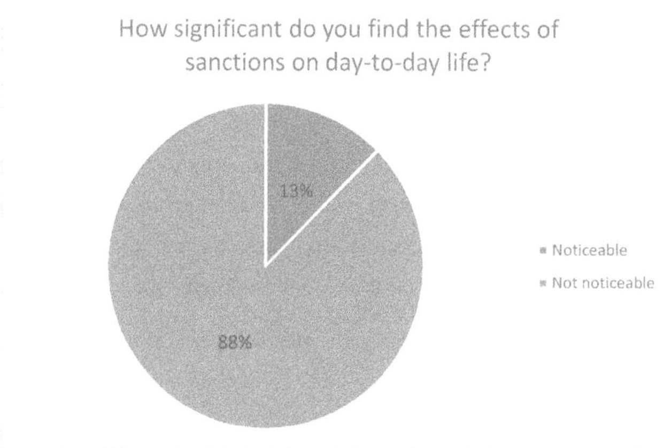

Question 3: How significant do you find the effects of sanctions on day-to-day life?

Surprisingly, merely 13% of the respondents (7) said that they find noticeable effects of sanctions on their day-to-day lives. An overwhelming majority, i.e. 88% of the respondents (49 out of 56) actually mentioned that the sanctions bear 'no noticeable' effects on their day-to-day lives.

This is a crucial evidence, which, significantly differs with the media rhetoric in the West that argues that the sanctions are achieving their intended foreign policy objectives, and are damaging the Russian economy to such a scale that is noticeable to average citizen and is making them disgruntled toward the current government.

Final words

Our findings and case studies on Russia, Iran, and Cuba depict that economic sanctions do not bear a significant impact on the target country's economy. Comprehensive analysis of macroeconomic indicators for aforementioned countries similarly suggest that while the countries might face a brief shock phase owing to the sanctions, this could be negated in mid-to long term by the target country by forming trade relations with other countries. An equal importance should be laid to the economic and geopolitical might of the target entity, since it plays crucial role in its ability to leverage its economic and political interests.

Taehee Whang[81] similarly points out that the sanctions on non-allies tend to have far lowers success rate, given their resistance and ability to quickly form trade relations with other non-allied entities.

Furthermore, a quantitative evidence through a cited published work also points out that the scope and extent of sanctions matter as well: United Nations-led sanctions seem to work far more extensively and do greater economic damage to the target country than the sanctions by the United States alone, for instance.

To conclude, international economic sanctions do not appear to achieve their foreign-policy objectives, and are often counterproductive to their intended effects. In fact, Dursun Peksen[82] argues that economic sanctions have a significant effect on human rights as well. Not only do they worsen the government respect for physical integrity rights, extensive sanctions have also been shown to be much more detrimental to the human rights than partial trade sanctions. Furthermore, economic sanctions remain a counterproductive policy tool.

---

[81] Whang, T. (2010). Structural estimation of economic sanctions: From initiation to outcomes. *Journal of Peace Research*, [online] 47(5), pp.561-573. Available at: http://www.jstor.org/stable/20798926 [Accessed 13 Jun. 2016].

[82] Peksen, D. (2009). Better or Worse? The Effect of Economic Sanctions on Human Rights. *Journal of Peace Research*, 46(1), pp.59-77.

Bibliography

In order as it appears in the text

1. http://www.un.org/en/globalissues/internationallaw/ (access date: 29.02.2016)
2. Al. Bolintineanu, A. Nastase, B. Aurescu (2000), International Public Law, Bucharest: All Beck Publishing House, p.258.
3. http://www.un.org/en/sections/un-charter/chapter-vii/index.html (access date: 29.02.2016)
4. Crăciunescu (2006), International Public Law, Concordia Publishing House, Arad, p. 252.
5. 'Sanctions' refer to 'economic sanctions' from this point onward.
6. Security Council Report, http://www.securitycouncilreport.org/atf/cf/%7B65BFCF9B-6D27-4E9C-8CD3-CF6E4FF96FF9%7D/special_research_report_sanctions_2013.pdf (access date: 29.02.2016)
7. Philip I. Levy (1999), Sanctions on South Africa: What Did They Do?, http://www.econ.yale.edu/growth_pdf/cdp796.pdf (access date: 29.02.2016)
8. http://www.bbc.com/news/business-35317159 (access date: 29.02.2016)
9. http://www.bbc.com/news/business-35398423 (access date: 29.02.2016)
10. euronews. (2016). Ukrainian opposition uses polls to bolster cause. [online] Available at: http://www.euronews.com/2013/12/13/ukrainian-opposition-uses-polls-to-bolster-cause/ [Accessed 4 May 2016].
11. 2001.ukrcensus.gov.ua. (2001). Всеукраїнський перепис населення 2001. [online] Available at: http://2001.ukrcensus.gov.ua/eng/results/general/nationality/ [Accessed 4 May 2016].

12. Rb.com.ua. (2012). Euromaydan - 2013. R&B Group. [online] Available at: http://rb.com.ua/eng/projects/omnibus/8840/ [Accessed 5 May 2016].

13. Kiis.com.ua. (2014). How relations between Ukraine and Russia should look like? Public opinion polls results. [online] Available at: http://www.kiis.com.ua/?lang=eng&cat=reports&id=236&page=1 [Accessed 6 May 2016].

14. International Republican Institute. (2014). Public Opinion Survey Residents of Ukraine. [online] Available at:http://www.iri.org/sites/default/files/2014%20April%205%20IRI%20Public%20Opinion%20Survey%20of%20Ukraine,%20March%2014-26,%202014.pdf [Accessed 5 May 2016].

15. Комментарии.ua, (2014). Одесский горсовет приготовился к штурму. [online] Available at: http://odessa.comments.ua/news/2014/01/26/214700.html [Accessed 7 May 2016].

16. Kyiv Post, (2014). What really happened in Odessa. [online] Available at: http://www.kyivpost.com/article/content/ukraine/what-really-happened-in-odessa-a-step-by-step-reconstruction-of-a-tragedy-that-killed-46-people-video-346192.html [Accessed 7 May 2016].

17. Украинская Правда. (2014). В Луганске участники "русской весны" захватили ОГА и просят у Путина ввести войска. [online] Available at: http://www.pravda.com.ua/rus/news/2014/03/2/7017106/ [Accessed 7 May 2016].

18. McElroy, D. (2014). Ukraine crisis: separatist in Donetsk proclaims 'people's government'. [online] Telegraph.co.uk. Available at: http://www.telegraph.co.uk/news/worldnews/europe/ukraine/10676785/Separatist-in-Donetsk-proclaims-peoples-government.html [Accessed 7 May 2016].

19. RT International. (2014). Crimea declares independence, seeks UN recognition. [online] Available at: https://www.rt.com/news/crimea-referendum-results-official-250/ [Accessed 8 May 2016].

20. Taylor, A. (2014). To understand Crimea, take a look back at its complicated history. [online] Washington Post. Available at: https://www.washingtonpost.com/news/worldviews/wp/2014/02/27/to-understand-crimea-take-a-look-back-at-its-complicated-history/ [Accessed 10 May 2016].

21. Zakon1.rada.gov.ua. (1991). Про відновлення Кримської Автономної Радянської Соціалістичної Республіки. [online] Available at: http://zakon1.rada.gov.ua/laws/show/712-12 [Accessed 10 May 2016].

22. Laura Smith-Spark. Phil Black and Frederik Pleitgen, C. (2014). Russia flexes military muscle as tensions rise in Ukraine's Crimea - CNN.com. [online] CNN. Available at: http://edition.cnn.com/2014/02/26/world/europe/ukraine-politics [Accessed 10 May 2016].

23. RT International. (2014). Crimea declares independence, seeks UN recognition. [online] Available at: https://www.rt.com/news/crimea-referendum-results-official-250/ [Accessed 10 May 2016].

24. Pew Research Center. (2014). Despite Concerns about Governance, Ukrainians want to remain one country. [online] Available at: http://www.pewglobal.org/files/2014/05/Pew-Global-Attitudes-Ukraine-Russia-Report-FINAL-May-8-2014.pdf [Accessed 9 May 2016].

25. Gibbons-Neff, T. (2015). The unusual difficulty of tracking Russia's dead in Ukraine and Syria. [online] Washington Post. Available at: https://www.washingtonpost.com/news/checkpoint/wp/2015/10/27/the-unusual-difficulty-of-tracking-russias-dead-in-ukraine-and-syria/ [Accessed 10 May 2016].

26. All Russian MPs volunteer to be subject to US, E. (2014). All Russian MPs volunteer to be subject to US, EU sanctions. [online] Sputniknews.com. Available at: http://sputniknews.com/voiceofrussia/news/2014_03_18/All-Russian-MPs-volunteer-to-be-subject-to-US-EU-sanctions-7889/ [Accessed 10 May 2016].

27. BBC News. (2014). How far do EU-US sanctions on Russia go? - BBC News. [online] Available at: http://www.bbc.com/news/world-europe-28400218 [Accessed 10 May 2016].

28. Newsroom - European Commission. (n.d.). EU sanctions against Russia over Ukraine crisis - Newsroom - European Commission. [online] Available at: http://europa.eu/newsroom/highlights/special-coverage/eu_sanctions_en [Accessed 10 May 2016].

29. Consilium.europa.eu. (2016). Timeline - EU restrictive measures in response to the crisis in Ukraine - Consilium. [online] Available at: http://www.consilium.europa.eu/en/policies/sanctions/ukraine-crisis/history-ukraine-crisis/ [Accessed 10 May 2016].

30. RT International. (2014). Sanctions tit-for-tat: Moscow strikes back against US officials. [online] Available at: https://www.rt.com/news/foreign-ministry-russia-sanctions-133/ [Accessed 10 May 2016].

31. Garant.ru. (2014). УКАЗ ПРЕЗИДЕНТА РФ ОТ 6 АВГУСТА 2014 Г. N 560 "О ПРИМЕНЕНИИ ОТДЕЛЬНЫХ СПЕЦИАЛЬНЫХ ЭКОНОМИЧЕСКИХ МЕР В ЦЕЛЯХ ОБЕСПЕЧЕНИЯ БЕЗОПАСНОСТИ РОССИЙСКОЙ ФЕДЕРАЦИИ". [online] Available at: http://www.garant.ru/hotlaw/federal/558039/ [Accessed 10 May 2016].

32. RAPSI. (2016). Russian authorities bust 5,000 tons of sanctioned food products since November - report. [online] Available at: http://rapsinews.com/news/20160425/275948715.html [Accessed 10 May 2016].

33. Ostroukh, A. (2014). Russia Ready to Float Ruble Next Year Regardless of Rate. [online] WSJ. Available at: http://www.wsj.com/news/articles/SB10001424052702304419104579326441407494108 [Accessed 12 May 2016].

34. Bloomberg.com. (2014). Russia Defends Ruble With Biggest Rate Rise Since 1998. [online] Available at: http://www.bloomberg.com/news/articles/2014-12-15/russia-increases-key-interest-rate-to-17-to-stem-ruble-decline [Accessed 12 May 2016].

35. Anderson, J. (2014). Ruble Crisis Is Testing Russia's Resources. [online] DealBook. Available at: http://dealbook.nytimes.com/2014/12/17/russian-government-tries-to-support-volatile-ruble/?_r=0 [Accessed 12 May 2016].

36. Atlas.cid.harvard.edu. (2016). What did Kazakhstan export in 2014? | The Atlas Of Economic Complexity. [online] Available at: http://atlas.cid.harvard.edu/explore/tree_map/export/kaz/all/show/2014/ [Accessed 15 May 2016].

37. The Moscow Times. (2016). Moscow's Apartment Market Down 30 Percent | News. [online] Available at: http://www.themoscowtimes.com/businessrealestate/article/moscows-apartment-market-down-30-percent/556280.html [Accessed 15 May 2016].

38. The Economist. (2014). Why China is creating a new "World Bank" for Asia. [online] Available at: http://www.economist.com/blogs/economist-explains/2014/11/economist-explains-6 [Accessed 16 May 2016].

39. RT. (2014). Russia-China 'Gas Deal of the century'. [online] Available at: https://www.rt.com/files/news/27/14/40/00/gas3.7.jpg [Accessed 16 May 2016].

40. Kramer, A. (2014). Russia's Steep Rate Increase Fails to Stem Ruble's Decline. [online] Nytimes.com. Available at: http://www.nytimes.com/2014/12/17/business/russia-ruble-interest-rates.html [Accessed 19 May 2016].

41. РБК. (2016). «Новая реальность»: о чем Герман Греф рассказал акционерам Сбербанка. [online] Available at: http://www.rbc.ru/finances/27/05/2016/574835599a7947103afd8ece [Accessed 19 May 2016].

42. Christie, E. (2015). Sanctions after Crimea: Have they worked?. [online] NATO Review. Available at: http://www.nato.int/docu/Review/2015/Russia/sanctions-after-crimea-have-they-worked/EN/index.htm [Accessed 15 May 2016].

43. Bershidsky, L. (2015). Saudi Arabia's Oil War With Russia. [online] Bloomberg View. Available at: http://www.bloomberg.com/view/articles/2015-10-16/saudi-arabia-s-oil-war-with-russia [Accessed 21 May 2016].

44. International Business Times. (2016). EU Unity Crumbles As Russia Sanctions Extension Debate Rages. [online] Available at: http://www.ibtimes.com/eu-unity-crumbles-russia-sanctions-extension-debate-rages-2376693 [Accessed 4 Jun. 2016].

45. Bloomberg.com. (2016). These Are the World's Most Innovative Economies. [online] Available at: http://www.bloomberg.com/news/articles/2016-01-19/these-are-the-world-s-most-innovative-economies [Accessed 20 May 2016].

46. IMF. (2016). World Economic Outlook. [online] Available at: http://www.imf.org/external/pubs/ft/weo/2016/update/01/pdf/0116.pdf [Accessed 17 May 2016].

47. World Bank. (2015). World Bank Keeps 2015 Growth Projections for Russia, and Slightly Revises 2016-2017 Outlook. [online] Available at: http://www.worldbank.org/en/news/press-release/2015/12/18/world-bank-keeps-2015-growth-projections-for-russia-and-slightly-revises-2016-2017-outlook [Accessed 19 May 2016].

48. Amnesty. (1978). Amnesty International Report, 1978. [online] Available at: https://www.amnesty.org/download/Documents/204000/pol100011978eng.pdf [Accessed 19 May 2016].

49. Bryne, M. (2013). CIA Admits It Was Behind Iran's Coup. [online] Foreign Policy. Available at: http://foreignpolicy.com/2013/08/19/cia-admits-it-was-behind-irans-coup/ [Accessed 19 May 2016].

50. YouTube. (2016). Imam Khomeini - The Man Who Changed The World | Iran & The West [Part 1/3]. [online] Available at: https://www.youtube.com/watch?v=FfrJ2rBobGs [Accessed 9 May 2016].

51. Historyguy.com. (2016). The History Guy: Iran-U.S. Hostage Crisis (1979-1981). [online] Available at: http://www.historyguy.com/iran-us_hostage_crisis.html [Accessed 23 May 2016].

52. Fisk, R. (2004). The Great War for civilization. London: Fourth Estate.

53. Roe, S. (2007). An atomic threat made in America. [online] chicagotribune.com. Available at: http://www.chicagotribune.com/news/nationworld/chi-061209atoms-day1-story,0,2034260.htmlstory [Accessed 18 May 2016].

54. IAEA. (2003). IAEA GOV/2003/40: Implementation of the NPT safeguards agreement in the Islamic Republic of Iran. [online] Available at: http://www.iaea.org/Publications/Documents/Board/2003/gov2003-40.pdf [Accessed 20 May 2016].

55. Samore, G. (2015). Sanctions Against Iran: A Guide to Targets, Terms, and Timetables. [online] Harvard Kennedy School. Available at: http://belfercenter.ksg.harvard.edu/files/Iran%20Sanctions.pdf [Accessed 18 May 2016].

56. Eia.doe.gov. (2016). Iran - U.S. Energy Information Administration (EIA). [online] Available at: http://www.eia.doe.gov/countries/cab.cfm?fips=IR [Accessed 19 May 2016].

57. Schweid, B. (2008). Iran Oil industry founders. [online] Seattle Times. Available at: http://seattletimes.nwsource.com/html/nationworld/2003494872_iranoil26.html [Accessed 19 May 2016].

58. Ec.europa.eu. (2016). Iran - Trade - European Commission. [online] Available at: http://ec.europa.eu/trade/creating-opportunities/bilateral-relations/countries/iran/ [Accessed 19 May 2016].

59. Indexmundi.com. (2010). Iran Inflation rate (consumer prices) - Economy. [online] Available at: http://www.indexmundi.com/iran/inflation_rate_(consumer_prices).html [Accessed 17 May 2016].

60. Cia.gov. (2016). The World Factbook. [online] Available at: https://www.cia.gov/library/publications/the-world-factbook/geos/ir.html [Accessed 19 May 2016].

61. France24. (2015). Iran Five Year Plan targets annual 8% growth. [online] Available at: http://www.france24.com/en/20100111-iran-five-year-plan-targets-annual-8-growth?quicktabs_1=0 [Accessed 19 May 2016].

62. latimes. (2012). Prices in Iran rise after lifting of subsidies. [online] Available at: http://www.latimes.com/news/nationworld/world/la-fg-iran-subsidies-20101223,0,5543095.story?track=rss [Accessed 19 May 2016].

63. Google Books. (2014). Energy and the Iranian economy : hearing. [online] Available at: https://books.google.com/books?id=CA1Cn8tDMv4C&pg=PA50&dq=iran+energy+superpower&hl=en&sa=X&ei=uBKYU6jJOabLsQT9y4DIDQ&ved=0CC0Q6AEwAw#v=onepage&q=energy%20superpower&f=false [Accessed 19 May 2016].

64. Seekingalpha.com. (2016). Iranian Sanctions Repealed - Focus On Natural Gas. [online] Available at: http://seekingalpha.com/article/3977759-iranian-sanctions-repealed-focus-natural-gas [Accessed 19 May 2016].

65. Seekingalpha.com. (2016). Middle East Stocks Crash On Iran Sanctions: ETFs To Watch. [online] Available at: http://seekingalpha.com/article/3826376-middle-east-stocks-crash-iran-sanctions-etfs-watch [Accessed 26 May 2016].

66. Reuters. (2014). For 23rd time, U.N. nations urge end to U.S. embargo on Cuba. [online] Available at: http://www.reuters.com/article/2014/10/28/us-cuba-un-idUSKBN0IH1RN20141028 [Accessed 25 May 2016].

67. Dur, P. and Gilcrease, C. (2002). US Diplomacy and the Downfall of a Cuban Dictator: Machado in 1933. Journal of Latin American Studies, [online] 34(02), pp.255-282. Available at: http://dx.doi.org/10.1017/S0022216X02006417 [Accessed 24 May 2016].

68. Olson, J. (2000). Historical dictionary of the 1950s. Westport, Conn.: Greenwood Press.

69. Grandin, G. and Joseph, G. (2010). A century of revolution. Durham [NC]: Duke University Press.

70. Archives.chicagotribune.com. (1960). Ike Slashes Sugar Quotas. [online] Available at: http://archives.chicagotribune.com/1960/07/07/page/1/article/ike-slashes-cuban-sugar-quota [Accessed 30 May 2016].

71. State.gov. (1992). Cuba Democracy Act. [online] Available at: http://www.state.gov/www/regions/wha/cuba/democ_act_1945.html [Accessed 23 May 2016].

72. Aljazeera.com. (2015). US and Cuba restore ties by opening embassies. [online] Available at: http://www.aljazeera.com/news/2015/07/cuba-restore-ties-opening-embassies-150720024721778.html [Accessed 25 May 2016].

73. Cia.gov. (2012). The World Factbook. [online] Available at: https://www.cia.gov/library/publications/the-world-factbook/geos/cu.html [Accessed 22 May 2016].

74. Zerohedge.com. (2016). Cuba – A History | Zero Hedge. [online] Available at: http://www.zerohedge.com/contributed/2014-05-06/cuba-%E2%80%93-history [Accessed 24 May 2016].

75. Pike, J. (2015). Cuba's Economy. [online] Globalsecurity.org. Available at: http://www.globalsecurity.org/military/world/cuba/economy.htm [Accessed 25 May 2016].

76. Teegen, H. (n.d.). Economic and Strategic Impacts of US Economic sanctions on Cuba. [online] George Washington University. Available at: https://www.gwu.edu/~clai/working_papers/Teegen_Hildy_02-03.pdf [Accessed 25 May 2016].

77. Reuters. (2016). Cuba economic growth rises to 4.7 pct in first half -minister. [online] Available at: http://www.reuters.com/article/2015/07/15/cuba-economy-idUSL2N0ZV1PR20150715 [Accessed 19 May 2016].

78. Texas A&M University. (2016). Emerging Markets for U.S. Agriculture: Focus on Cuba. [online] Available at: http://cnas.tamu.edu/Publications/E312.pdf [Accessed 30 May 2016].

79. Hufbauer, G. (2007). Economic sanctions reconsidered. Washington, DC: Peterson Institute for International Economics.

80. Neuenkirch, M. and Neumeier, F. (2014). The Impact of UN and US Economic Sanctions on GDP Growth. [online] Marburg Centre for Institutional Economics •. Available at: https://www.uni-marburg.de/fb02/macie/research/output/macie/neuenkirch_neumeier_2014_2.pdf [Accessed 8 Jun. 2016].

81. Whang, T. (2010). Structural estimation of economic sanctions: From initiation to outcomes. Journal of Peace Research, [online] 47(5), pp.561-573. Available at: http://www.jstor.org/stable/20798926 [Accessed 13 Jun. 2016].

82. Peksen, D. (2009). Better or Worse? The Effect of Economic Sanctions on Human Rights. Journal of Peace Research, 46(1), pp.59-77.

www.ingramcontent.com/pod-product-compliance
Lightning Source LLC
La Vergne TN
LVHW021114300926
849160LV00009B/733
* 9 7 8 3 9 6 0 6 7 0 9 7 1 *